DATE DUE

NOV 2 6 1979			
MAY 4 1981			
MAY 2 5 1981			
JUN 4 1981			
4-21-82			
JAN 1 3 1986			
MAR 1 1 2000			
GAYLORD 234			PRINTED IN U. S. A.

fifty plus

BY Jeanette Lockerbie

Tomorrow's at My Door
The Image of Joy
"Just Take It From the Lord, Brother"
The Dino Story (WITH Dino Kartsonakis)
Fifty Plus

How recycling your potential *now* can
mean a joyous and fulfilled tomorrow

Jeanette Lockerbie
fifty plus

16887

Fleming H. Revell Company
Old Tappan, New Jersey

Scripture quotations not otherwise identified are from the King James Version of the Bible.

Scripture quotations identified LB are from The Living Bible, Copyright © 1971 by Tyndale House Publishers, Wheaton, Illinois 60187. All rights reserved.

Excerpts from "Tomorrow Unlimited" and "The Gift of Today and Tomorrow" are from *Tomorrow's at My Door* by Jeanette Lockerbie, Copyright © 1973 by Fleming H. Revell Co. and used by permission.

Excerpt from "A Prayer for Older Folks" is from *Coping with Loneliness* by Inez Spence. Copyright 1970 by Baker Book House Company. Used with permission.

Excerpt from "Old Phones Never Quit Ringing" is by Les Goldberg, appeared in the *Herald-Examiner* (9/21/75) and is reprinted courtesy *Los Angeles Herald-Examiner*.

Excerpt from "Letting the Retired Man Be a Man" by Jeanette Lockerbie, which appeared in *Psychology for Living*, is used with permission of the Narramore Christian Foundation, Rosemead, California 91770.

Library of Congress Cataloging in Publication Data

Lockerbie, Jeanette W
   Fifty plus.

   1. Middle age—Religious life. 2. Retirement.
I. Title.
BV4579.5.L6   248'.84   76–6939
ISBN 0–8007–0793–1

FOR *my family—*
Your supportive belief in me,
together with God's unfailing
help, made it possible for me
to recycle at fifty plus.

Contents

Preface

A book, like a baby, has a definable beginning, a pinpoint conception. This book evolved from the deliberate nudging of one Christian challenging another to "Recycle, man!" Even while I filed away the conversation (in which I had a part) to repeat verbatim to the person for whom it was intended, the ink-driven wheels were beginning to turn in my mind. *Recycling.* It's with us and is a part of our thinking in today's society.

A trash heap. Tin cans—flattened, dented, rusted as though they had been there a long time—or shiny ones looking like new arrivals on the junk pile. Whatever their appearance they have one thing in common. They have outlived their usefulness.

Some people feel that they have outlived their usefulness, that they are life's discards. They feel relegated to the graveyard of hope and dreams and expectations. They are the retired, the bereaved, the divorced or deserted, the chronically ill or handicapped, the capable who have been replaced by a machine. The *disrupted,* for whatever the reason.

At any age, any one of these conditions can spell catastrophe. To the FIFTY PLUS person it presents its unique age-related crisis—and the individual may feel more and more eligible for life's scrap heap. This is even more accentuated in the mid-seventies because, in the words of Alvin Toffler in *Future Shock,* "We have developed a throw-away mentality to match our throw-away products." We have almost buried ourselves in our throwaways, in our garbage. But—and this is a great big shiny neon light "but"—the same prodigal society that has produced veritable mountains of toss-away material has, commendably, also launched and propagated the phenomenon of *recycling.*

9

If, in the interests of self-preservation, it is crucial that we reverse the "discard" mind-set and practice, how much more do we need to emphasize and practice the recycling of human potential? *That is what this book is about.*

Tin cans, bottles, old newspapers, and magazines have in them the makings of perennially needed goods. *People*—men and women who are fifty plus—also have value yet to be reckoned with. How to recycle their skills, their talents, their know-how and experience in a world that will never have a sufficiency of such resources? This is what we hope to come to grips with in these chapters. Among the considerations are:

- What prevents people from seeing the future as theirs?
- Why should the forcibly retired have feelings of inferiority which keep them from recycling?
- How can a seeming irreversible loss be a stepping-stone to fulfillment?
- What are the opportunities available to the fifty plus?
- When *are* "the best years of our lives"?

God has no retirement scrap heap. He has ordained that we should still be fruitful—whatever our age. It is my sincere desire that in reading this book you will become excited about activating a dream, finishing a long-delayed project, enjoying the *today* which is the first day of the rest of your life.

fifty plus

1

The Tyranny of Retirement

If you no longer look ahead,
If your ambitions' fires are dead—
Then you are old.

Author unknown

With a flip of the calendar the day arrives—for better or for worse. Whether retirement is voluntary or mandated, how the new retiree accepts it is not determined when he actually reaches this milestone. Rather, we are programming ourselves, sometimes for years, for this reaction. Consciously or unconsciously we are building an attitude toward retirement.

Some people are quite outspoken about it. For example, I was speaking to a group of teachers on the topic, "Being the Kind of Teacher You Really Want to Be," and for starters I asked that the group share with each other and with me their ideas on the subject. Without hesitation a woman spoke up. "I'd like to be a *retired* teacher," she said. It would have been interesting to learn what factors had fed into that desire, for she was not being facetious.

The reactions to the arrival of retirement speak volumes about the person. For retirement does come, whatever we might think about it. Some people have prepared emotionally and practically for their retirement years. They are the happy ones, for they are retiring not *from* but *to* something. Their futures stretch before them with purpose and challenge and color. I know such a couple. Just a day or so ago I received a note from them that spoke of the husband's retirement:

"That chapter is closed and we can hardly wait for the next adventures."

This is a healthy attitude. Perhaps it is more prevalent with people who have some choice as to when they will retire. They may opt for early retirement with a view to recycling. Not waiting to be acted upon by circumstances, they are the activators. They may have taken seriously a certain commercial dealing with cans and bottles: "Recycling Begins With You."

Unquestionably, retirement time is a human crisis—and a crisis notoriously brings out both the best and the worst in us. It is interesting to me that in the Chinese language the word for *crisis* and the word for *opportunity* is the same. Some see retirement only as a tyrant against which they are helpless. Others, the happy retirees, view it as an opportunity for new experiences and adventures.

The unhappy retiree seems to feel that life has virtually come to an end for him. One person I interviewed lamented, "They might as well have handed me my death warrant; I'd as soon be dead as have to give up my position." Here is a woman who had never really faced the fact that this would happen to her. Like many others of retirement age, she was in excellent physical shape; her mind was alert. Tests would have shown she was never more equipped in every sense to fill the position that she must now relinquish.

It takes a particular quality of maturity for one to keep serene and accepting when confronted with being put on the shelf. Some don't make it. Even though they have known for years that it was coming, retirement just makes them feel resentful and resistant. They see themselves as having put the best years of their lives into becoming what they mentally and experientially are in their profession or business. This frustration may be fanned by the knowledge that they are being replaced by someone not only younger but—however highly trained—lacking the background of experience. It is especially galling and hard to take when the replacement is a *machine*. Many men and women are being superannuated by a computer. Frustration turns to bitterness and the person may become unreasonable about the situation.

All too often, in a kind of protest, they resort to doing nothing. Add to this their outraged pride and their feelings of self-pity—and such people are in deep trouble emotionally. It is difficult to rouse them from their Slough of Despond, and in a remarkably short time deterioration sets in: physical, mental, and yes, spiritual. Christians are not immune to these reactions. There is something in a person's inability to accept what has happened in the natural course of things which is akin to turning down God's sovereignty in his life. It is as though his faith has reached its limits; he feels he has no tomorrow.

Meanwhile the unhappy retiree is passing up opportunities for genuine fulfillment. Perhaps (subconsciously, at least) he or she is saying, "I've been rejected for the job I know I can do well. Why should I look for anything else and risk being turned down?" So he never finds out the satisfaction and gratification which can come to one who takes a chance and recycles.

Generally, the opportunities, while they *are* available, have to be sought. The door marked OPPORTUNITY does not have a person's name stamped on it. It has to be pushed open. So it is sad when the fact of retirement causes a person to feel inferior, to think, *Who would want me?* It is not hard to empathize with this kind of thinking, for with the mere turning of a page of the calendar, the man or woman has become less, in his own thinking, than he was the day before. The alarm rings—but there is no urgency about heeding it. The school bell rings—but for the retired teacher to whom the schoolroom was her world this is sheer trauma.

Attitude is the key to reaction. The man or woman who has sensibly and objectively faced up to the inevitable sixty-five will have a balanced attitude toward retirement. We will never seek nor recognize and grasp recycling opportunities until we have the positive attitude that life has more for us, that the future is ours.

Perhaps, like Dr. Martin Luther King, we need a dream throughout life. We often cannot choose the means of earning a living, and many people go through life dragging themselves to work, year in and year out—and hating their jobs. We can, however, visualize what we would like to do with our lives and activate that dream in retirement. Just having that vision, we can be taking steps to prepare in the right direction and be ready for the opportunity when it knocks. The very fact of having such a preoccupation with something tremendously meaningful can take the sting out of forced retirement and change it from a tyrant to a friend who makes possible the fulfillment of a dream.

What comes to the retired person who recycles? Great personal satisfaction and a sense of fulfillment. Frequently he is meeting a need that would otherwise not be met. His total outlook on life is changed. Retirement is just a pause on the landing of life before starting up another flight.

Away then with feelings of dejection and rejection and, as that friend of mine advised an old college buddy, "Recycle, man!"

First, you have to "think" recycle, not "Why *should* I recycle?" We used to hear that "You are what you eat." Recent studies show that a person's well-being may also depend on how he thinks. This is not news to one who is familiar with the New Testament. Long ago the Apostle Paul prescribed a mind-menu for equanimity:

> . . . Fix your thoughts on what is true and good and right. Think about things that are pure and lovely, and dwell on the fine, good things in others. Think about all you can praise God for and be glad about.
>
> Philippians 4:8 LB

Such thinking makes for happiness, and scientists at Duke University have found that a higher "happiness" rating coincides with a longer life for the older people they studied.

"The decision to have an active mental, physical, and social life is the important decision," said one doctor. "It's saying 'yes' to life."

This is throwing your own challenge into the face of retirement, robbing it of its tyranny over you.

2

When You Run Out of a Future

While there is still time, learn to deal with yourself and you can deal with life.

Roy W. Menninger

Some people, women in particular, run out of a future when the last child is grown and gone from the home. It may be that this has been your experience:

The wedding is over. You are back from the reception. You just sit down to catch your breath after the days and weeks of hectic, happy activity. A few friends are with you and you beam as you listen for the dozenth time to "I never saw a more beautiful bride!" (*Of course not,* you think. *She's my daughter,* or, *My son picked her.*) The talk goes on and on about the lovely wedding ceremony, till the guests have finally gone.

In a day or so the house is back to normal. *Normal?* you think ruefully. *With my last child gone from the home! Normal? With a great gaping emptiness in my life!*

Is it *normal* not to have a daughter or son calling downstairs, "Mom, please do this or that for me; I'm in an awful hurry"?

Is it *normal* not to have them monopolize the telephone or the bathroom and fill the house with their jolly, noisy, hungry friends?

Frequently the mother sighs and weeps inwardly, feeling that life will never be the same. She resigns herself to a kind of half-life. How well I remember the day my son rode off with his lovely bride, properly leaving his father and his mother to cleave to the girl he had chosen as his life's mate.

And can I ever forget the December day when, through a ghostlike fog, a ship sailed out of Vancouver harbor? A ship carrying my only daughter half a world away to the mission field. "God gives grace for such experiences," I had long heard and personally asserted. Oh, but it is so different when it is your own daughter! God did not forsake us—her father and me—as we watched that ship steam too speedily for us to keep up along the dockside. But I confess that my spirits matched the bleakness of the day.

No. I had not run out of a future, but I did have a gap in my life.

This is normal. It would be a poor sort of mother who did not greatly miss her child who no longer comes home every day, even though from the day children are born, every plan or dream for them has in it the seeds of their leaving home someday. Still, as mothers we are not prepared—ever. Few of us are so mature as to realize that "I'm not less a mother just because I am not so much needed."

Actually this severing begins the day a child starts school. (All you have to do is listen to a kindergarten teacher telling how much trouble she has with the *mothers.*) When the son or daughter goes off to college, the problem is really accentuated for many mothers—and dads, too. This is when our children really leave home; nothing is ever quite the same again, no matter how often they may come home for a while.

I hope my Jeannie will pardon this illustration. She was very young, not yet seventeen, when she entered Methodist Hospital School of Nursing just a few miles from home. She had not been in training many months when one weekend she said to me, "Mother, it's hard to be your little girl when I come home on the weekend, when all week *people's lives have been depending on me.*" I smiled at the time. Looking back, I hear what she was actually saying then; she was telling me, "Let go, mother; I'm a big girl."

Such a difficult lesson for us to learn. Such a rude awakening not to be needed after getting ourselves set in this mold. But, like every other situation with which we are confronted, it has to be faced. The cases of the mother who seemingly cannot adjust to this perfectly natural circumstance are legion. And hers is a particularly virulent form of neurosis. And again self-pity is a key derivative, with depression in its wake. "See what my daughter has done to me," the mother moans, or, "How could my son go off and leave me—after all I've done for my children!"

We could all take a lesson from the Bible's story of the mother eagle. She "stirs up her nest," encouraging the young to try their own wings (*see* Deuteronomy 32:11). She is there, fluttering around and ready to save them if they would fall. But once they have proven their wings are strong enough to bear them, they are on their own. It is not recorded that the mother eagles get together and lament that the nests are empty, since it is a natural expectation.

One day, interacting with a psychologist on this problem so common to mothers, I was more than a little interested in a concept he submitted. The psychologist, Dr. Wayne Caldwell, brought to light something that had never occurred to me, although it immediately made sense. And, by the way, I am indebted to him for the phrase "running out of a future," which also intrigued me.

"It's not always that the mother is grieving because she so greatly misses her daughter [or her son]: sometimes the fact is that she no longer has them to manipulate. And when the last one is gone, this is her great problem. She feels she's run out of a future *because she has no one left to manipulate.* "

Many of us know of a widow or widower who—lonely and unhappy —attempts to manipulate and control the lives of the married children. The result is usually alienation—he or she literally runs out of both family and friends who will put up with the childish and unrealistic expectations and maneuvering.

Our family members do not love us less because they need us less than they once did. They will love us *more* if we recognize their rights and quit demanding ours and manipulating them in order to get our own way. Manipulating savors of the kid who has a ball when the others playing with him don't have one. Unless he can have everything his own way, he may stamp his foot and say, "All right. If you won't play my way, I'll take my ball and go home." If we think this is obnoxious behavior in a child—well, you fill in what you think when it is a grown man or woman you are dealing with. Happily, such people are not in the majority.

I am thinking (and I smile, even as I remember) of a woman— "Grandma Crook" my children called her—who used to come and stay for days at a time with us. She loved to care for our home and free me to go visiting and help in the church work, and she was a delight to have around. I can sometimes hear her warm Lancashire accent even now. But we had competition! Her sons and daughters-in-law so loved having her with them that they vied with each other for her visits. Those were the days when a dime was worth something: churches had mission dime banks. Knowing her love for the Lord and for the church, the sons and the in-laws would bribe this mother. "We'll fill your missionary bank," they would coax, "if you'll come and stay a week or two." The Lord took her to be with Himself rather suddenly, and her going left a whole circle of family and friends feeling that someone special had gone out of their lives. She didn't have to manipulate anyone, and she never ran out of a future.

There is a Bible verse you will come across a number of times in this book. (Maybe you will memorize it and even be energized by it before you have finished.) Here it is:

> For I know the plans I have for you, says the Lord. They are plans for good and not for evil, to give you a future and a hope.
>
> Jeremiah 29:11 LB

Isn't that good to know? God has no scrap heaps. He deals in futures—and frequently this calls for recycling.

True, a loneliness comes when our children leave us for their own homes or whatever in life takes them to another place. There is no need to deny this. God never asks us to deny our deep feelings. "For he knoweth our frame . . ." (Psalms 103:14). He gave us our emotions.

We do ourselves and our children a disfavor, however, when we allow ourselves to dwell on other days and wish them back. How much better to commit the family to the Lord and commit our own future to Him, asking Him to make us useful. Who knows? God may have a greater ministry for you than was possible when your children needed you. God is interested in recycling your potential. All He needs is your willing cooperation. And if He guides you as He has guided me these past few years—you are in for an exciting time!

You have not run out of a future.

3

The Freedom of Being Yourself

To be what we are, and to become what we are capable of becoming, is the only end of life.

Robert Louis Stevenson

Is there really a light at the end of the tunnel of grief?

It would be hard to convince a person who is in this tunnel. In fact, at some points it would be almost cruel to suggest such a possibility, for grief, whatever the cause of it, must run its course in order to do its work in our lives. Recycling, moving into a new future, is the *last* thing a person wants to hear about while the hurt is fresh and raw.

Nevertheless, as hundreds of men and women will testify, as they look back they can discern that it was the very crisis itself, the loss of a significant person in their lives, that gave them the chance to be themselves. For some people this is the very first chance—no, not the first: in infancy we all have that opportunity—the freedom to be who we are. It is a short-lived state, to be sure, for life's necessary inhibitions soon take over. Parental "Do's and Don'ts" begin to mold even the tiny baby. Maybe earlier than we think, a baby can be picking up the vibrations—perhaps through a look or a tone of voice—of what is expected of him or her. The young child catches on to what is acceptable and can keep life relatively smooth. As we know, some conform; some never do.

Every stage of life imposes other people's expectations upon us, and to a greater or lesser degree we recognize this and try to fit the image. There is the teacher with her image of what the pupil should be, the peer-group image that teenagers live by, employer/employee expectations to be attained—and so it goes all through life. Even the husband and wife in more cases than not (as studies show) are rarely themselves. Always there is the "right" image, the "should" to be adhered to. Until—and for most people this is a tragic "until"—there is not a someone to whom it is genuinely meaningful *how* or *if* you fit the image.

And it is then hard to feel that there is anything left to live for.

Yet the time does come for most people (unless they had other deep disturbances in addition to the loss of the person dear to them) when they can catch at least a glimmer of light in the distance. And even this flickering candle spells hope.

When this moment arrives two questions are usually uppermost in the awakened consciousness: *Where am I going?* and *What am I going to do?* But underlying each of these is the bigger, philosophical question: *Who am I?*

These feelings are not always expressed, even in our thoughts. More often we tend to push them down. As Christians, we seem to have a sense that it is unspiritual to question, that this is not acceptable to God. Yet God is the Giver of our power to question, as He is of every other faculty we possess. He even bids us to "come and reason together" (*see* Isaiah 1:18).

Who am I? Where am I going? Why am I here?

At the risk of being considered simplistic, let me share with you my own unalterable belief that God has a plan for my life. He has a plan for your life, for the life of everyone who has trusted Jesus Christ and received Him as Lord and Saviour. So that is the answer to why I am here. This may be hard for you to accept at a particular time, if your life is being channeled in other directions than those which check out with your own plans for your life.

A young woman told me recently as we were talking along these lines, "I'm mad at God these days." Why was she angry at God? Because of certain things that had happened in her life, and she was not seeing God immediately clear up the whole thing and let her get on with what she really wanted to do with her life. Most of us are not all that honest and quick to admit it, but I suspect that, like myself, many Christians have such moments at particular junctures in life.

What does all this have to do with the recycling of our potential when life has completely changed our course? Actually, the questioning period can be the quickening of new life after years of what has been merely existing, getting through the days rather than living them. If I had never come to such a crossroads, I would not know what *does, does not,* and *can* happen to a person. I am just an average woman, so what happened to me could well be the experience of others who are themselves at one of life's "wits' end" corners.

How true the Bible is, in my experience. I had often read and even memorized the verse: "For our light affliction, which is but for a moment, works for me" (*see* 2 Corinthians 4:17). But I well remember the day I stopped at the word *work.* Who ever heard of trials and troubles working for anybody! But that is what the Bible says. And since, with God's always-available help, I have been proving this in my own life, some people have even said to me, "You know, you're much more of a person than you used to be. I always used to see you as a kind of mousy preacher's wife just shaking hands with people at the church door—not much else, just a shadowy person."

This frank appraisal did not disturb me one bit, for I had been content and happy to be in the shadow of an extremely personable preacher husband. He was impressive enough for both of us. But I think I understand what these people were saying. I had not been, as we hear a lot these days, "my own person"—myself.

It took me quite a long time to face up to the change in my life status with my husband's going since a whole lot of other things went out of my life. No longer was there the parsonage with its security, with the *belonging,* or the interest and concern of a whole congregation, the feeling of being special to them that loving parishioners had given me for so many years. Let me say that I had never at any time felt imposed upon, or that our family lived in a fishbowl or that church members unduly intruded on our private lives. I thoroughly reveled in my role of pastor's wife (however mousy I may have appeared). It was all the harder, then, for me to accept that this was all over and that all the pretending I might do would never make it the same again. Apart from the emotional tearing up that such a loss brings, there is the very real matter of physical survival and how to earn a living with —as was true in my own case—few marketable skills in a highly competitive world.

I can never fully express how good the Lord has been—and is—to me. When I needed it most He caused to surface a latent ability with which He had gifted me. In a true and deep sense it is in this work, professional writing, that I have found answers to who I am. And because of this I have learned to *be* who I am. How liberating, how freeing to the human spirit this is! *Freeing,* in that I am not trying to fit an image. I have found and I keep on discovering that once this compulsion to be what "they" think you should be is erased, you do not need the props of pretense.

Before any of this can occur, before recycling can begin to be a positive experience, there has to be this total recognition that the life you have been used to is no more. Lingering at the gate of the home that once was yours can only perpetuate unhappiness. Regretful looking back just impedes your progress, though admittedly it is hard not to fall prey to what-might-have-been or what-once-was sighing.

You have to say—and ask God to help you grasp the significance of what you are saying: "I am *not* the preacher's wife"—"I am *not* the woman waiting for her husband to come home for dinner"—"I am *not* the mother with my children still depending on me." Or, for the retiree: "I am *not* in charge of a department [a classroom, a business office, or whatever filled your life prior to retirement]."

There is a great plus for the person who can then begin to be himself. I even toy with the concept that it is at such a point in one's maturity that God can reactivate and work out His Plan A in a life. When we can appropriate sufficient grace (always there for the taking), when we can summon the will to even *thank* God for our circumstances, we are on the road to enjoying the good things His plan includes. How can we be sure they are good? Here's that verse again:

> For I know the plans I have for you, says the Lord. They are
> plans for good and not for evil, to give you a future and a hope.
> Jeremiah 29:11 LB

A *future* and a *hope?* If this were a singing commercial making its exaggerated promises, I wouldn't blame you for some cynical response. But this is God. He has plans for you, good plans—and for your good. I had good reason to believe this even before I found the verse in Jeremiah. This is the kind of God we have. But I am glad He spelled it out for us.

It makes sense that God has a plan for each individual. It figures that He has some special thing for you and me to do. Something that no one else is equally capable of doing. Why? Because each of us is unique; we are each *one of a kind.* When God made us He threw away the individual molds. God deals only in originals.

One day I took some friends to visit the famous Huntington Library in San Marino. At the entrance to the main art galleries I reminded one of our party that she would get to see the original Gainsborough's *The Blue Boy.* Hearing me, a uniformed attendant added, "Every one of our paintings is an original." I felt justly squelched.

In a far more significant sense, however, each human being is an original. God the Originator is the Creator of billions of people—and no two are alike. We use individual fingerprints as proof. But increasingly unique features unfold, none more meaningful than the individual thought processes. God does not make carbon copies and when, as seems likely, man will "reproduce himself" in a mechanical wonder-being, it will lack the very components that would qualify it as man. It will not be made in God's image, and will not be unique—exact copies will be possible.

On Layman's Sunday in the church I attend, the speaker was World Vision's vice-president, Dr. Engstrom. In the context of his sermon he exclaimed with great enthusiasm, "God doesn't deal in duplicates; there's only one Ted Engstrom!"

It follows, then, that since God has taken such care to make us individuals He must have a blueprint for your life and mine. Because this means so very much to me, I included the concept in these lines in my book of poems *Tomorrow's At My Door:*

Tomorrow Unlimited

I'm special to God
There is only one me
I lift my head high at the prospect.
Not a piece or a pawn,
I'm a part of God's plan
And the blueprint He holds. . . .

It is exciting to realize this, and I have long been impressed with the Bible verse:

> For we are his workmanship, created in Christ Jesus unto good works, which God hath before ordained. . . .
>
> Ephesians 2:10

God-ordained work. A specific work for each one of us. That should take care of the plaintive "Why am I here?" Having a job to do that no one else in all the world is so uniquely equipped to do—shouldn't this add dignity to what we work at? Shouldn't it cause us to hold up our heads? Does it not make life worth something? Yet, so often, when life deals us what we consider at the time a knockout blow, how we are prone to cry out, "Life's just not worth living."

The antidote to such debilitating thinking, obviously, can be the recognition that God does have an assignment for us, whatever we might think of our potential. "I see people every day who have abilities I do not have," writes Charles L. Allen. "But when I realize that God made me as I am for a special purpose, there is no reason for me to resent the fact that He made other people for different purposes."

This author has expressed exactly what I have discovered for myself in my recycling process. There is no more liberating concept than this, that *God made us what we are, to accomplish His design for us.* When this truth sank into my consciousness I stopped having envious feelings about some people's ability to do things I could never even approximate. I recognized that they have their talents and I have mine; that they came from the same Source, and that with our varied abilities we have corresponding responsibilities.

"Fine," you might be parrying, "but what if I don't ever find out where my talents lie. What can I do at this crossroads where the props have fallen from under me? How do you propose I should carry out God's plan for my life?"

That is a fair and sensible question and for each person the "how" is different. One cannot arbitrarily tell another, "This is what you should do," or, "I feel God would have you do this. God would not be what we know Him to be—the God who is Love, who is Light and who is Truth—if He played games with us. God does not tease; He does not tantalize, dangling promises before our eyes and then not keeping them. That is man's way at times, but never God's way. He has said in His Word: "Ask—and you will receive. Seek—and you will find. Knock—and it will be opened to you" (*see* Matthew 7:7).

It all begins with asking. When we ask, we are admitting our own insufficiency and this puts us right in line for God's sufficiency. Sound pious or preachy? It is neither. It is God's method of directing us when we really want His direction. I believe that God delights in revealing Himself and His will to us. I have a friend who says, "You have to want God's will desperately, to get it." That would speak of a crisis situation such as creates the need for recycling. I go along with this friend's thinking for it is the very nature of human beings to muddle along "doing it myself" and not seeking God's will and His help until stringent circumstances drive us to it. It is then, generally, that we quit window-shopping with regard to God's will, and get serious about it.

Sometimes God answers our asking and our seeking by calling into play some natural talent. This is what happened in my case: I had always been admiring of writers, to the point of awe; and while I might have vaguely dreamed of how wonderful it would be to write a book, I had never visualized myself as capable of even beginning such a thing!

I like to share with young people a saying of Dr. Clyde Narramore. It has equally great value for a person at any age who is faced with the necessity of breaking into the labor market. "Your natural abilities are God's suggestions for your life's work," says this noted psychologist.

This made sense to me the first time I heard it, and I still think it does. We unquestionably do better and with greater ease the thing for which we have some natural ability. This means that we can usually realize a measure of success in this area. Big successes are built on small ones, and the fact is that even a small success is ego building (much needed in the person who has suffered a shattering blow of any kind and who may because of it feel worthless). It is then that success in one area helps our confidence to reach out and try other new things. When our work pleases and we begin to receive approbation, the message comes across not only that what we do is okay, but that "*I am okay*." And that is a good feeling.

I can still remember the tingle, the almost unbearable excitement of receiving that acceptance of my first manuscript. I was alone that day and I couldn't wait to share this wonderful development in my life with an empathetic somebody. And I found one down the street.

For most people, acceptance of something we have created (or otherwise been responsible for) says, "I *am* somebody; I am worthwhile; I have value," and this leads to "I *can.*" It helps when someone whose opinion you value comes along and underlines what the publisher (in my case) has said in response to your initial try. Amazingly, in the very same mail as that first acceptance came a letter from my son and in it this suggestion: "Mother, your life must be rather empty [and he explained why he thought so]. Why don't you try professional writing? I know you can do it."

This calls to mind another warm little scene. It was my birthday, and my daughter, Jeannie, was home for the weekend from her nursing school. She picked up the mail and, waving a little magazine in her hand, called airily, "Mother, a *by-line* on your *birthday!*" It was indeed. Just a back-page item, but it was the first writing I had published. My name was on it. I was on my way. I was tasting the first fruits of the freedom to be myself.

To the person whose circumstances make it mandatory for you to create a new future for yourself, I offer these suggestions for recycling:

1. *Consider* (sit down and take time for this): "What do I enjoy doing most?"

2. *Probe further:* "If nothing prevented me, if I could choose my own vocation, what would I choose to spend my life doing?"

3. *Ask:* "How prepared am I for such work?" and objectively evaluate your ability in the direction of your preference.

4. *Contemplate:* "Am I willing to further my training if need be?" (I should interject here that at the very first opportunity after discovering my writing gift I began to study the craft, and still take every opportunity to sharpen my skills.)

5. *Start each day by thanking God* for the gift He has given you, then humbly offer it back to God for Him to bless and increase. This is the most important tip one person could ever give another. It is the core secret of the success I have known. Starting the day with this good relationship with the Lord energizes my mind and frees the flow of the creativity juices. This is true whatever the area of your talent.

6. *Believe in yourself.* A woman I know has come a long way in believing in herself. She used to be so insecure and self-effacing—but

she worked on this area in her life, sought God's help, and came to realize that, far from being a nobody, she was one of God's somebodies. A fine worker, she had never really reached her potential. Then one day she applied for a new position. At the end of the questionnaire given her to fill out was this question: "Why, in your opinion, should you be given this position?"

Without hesitation she wrote: "I feel you can do no better than hire me. I'm qualified and I'm dependable and my work record will prove this."

She got the job—because she believed in herself. This is one of the great plus factors when you know the freedom of being yourself.

It can make all the difference in your recycling process.

4

How **Can** *I Thank God?*

Thanking God says, "Though I don't understand, I know You are in loving control."

Death. Divorce. Desertion. Who is to say which of the traumatic three is the worst to bear?

Two women were sympathizing with each other in their aloneness. One had been recently widowed and she badly needed someone who would let her talk and who would really listen to her minutely detailed account of her husband's death. At one point the other woman sighed and half-whispered, "There are some things worse than a good clean death." Her husband had deserted her for another woman. "And some people are telling me I should just thank the Lord, trust Him, and keep on going," she added wearily.

Death and desertion. Some time ago I was speaking at a women's retreat where the topic given me was "The Conquering Power of Praise." In our first session I suggested that each woman think about it and write down one thing for which she could *not* praise God at that time. We then had a sharing time. Later, in private, one of the women elaborated to me on the one thing for which she felt she could not praise God.

"My husband doesn't want our marriage any longer. He's started divorce proceedings," she told me, "and how *can* I thank God for this?"

What could I say? My heart ached for her.

"In every thing give thanks," we had discussed earlier, and "Who-ever offers praise glorifies me," and "His praise shall *continually* be in my mouth" (*see* 1 Thessalonians 5:18; Psalms 50:23; 34:1).

Yes, thank God for the death of the one who means everything in the world to you. The awful finality of it—the loss of lover, protector, provider, daily companion, and partner in life's adventures. Thank God for all this loss!

Thank God for divorce or desertion—with the associated emotional clobbering, the ego shattering, the feelings of failure and guilt engendered (in addition to the physical and material deprivation often suffered by the widowed). Thank God for all of these!

Bible truth. And this was an avowed Christian woman. Nevertheless, few people, *while* they are going through a severe trial, want to be told to "just praise the Lord." Nor will a sensitive Christian spray such phrases around at such a time.

Another tack the thoughtful, concerned fellow Christian will not take is: "I know why this has come into your life; the Lord wants to do something for you and this is His way of bringing it to pass." This, too, might very well be true, for trials and problems are a part of God's plan for most of us, and somehow, *in time,* we can almost come to the place where we actually thank God for heartache and pain. But at the time—no—unless you are made of far better spiritual stuff than I am (which you may be).

It takes a powerful measure of spiritual maturity to ride the waves when you lose your life's partner—whether by death, desertion, or divorce. Most people flounder, for a while at least. And possibly the very last thing they want to hear is: "Just thank the Lord."

"To every thing there is a season . . ." (Ecclesiastes 3:1). There is a time to quote Scripture, and there is a time to console by other means. Even so, things go better with *thanks.*

There are at least two reasons why this is so. First, the Bible bids us: "In every thing give thanks: for this is the will of God . . . concerning you" (1 Thessalonians 5:18)—and obedience brings its own reward. Second, God has promised to be with us in trouble; we can thank Him for that.

I have long been impressed that we are to give thanks *in* trouble, not *for* it (that would be rubbing salt into a wound and God is not like that). Also, God has promised to keep us while we are *in the midst* of trouble (*see* Psalms 138:7), not to keep us from ever having troubles.

"We don't like to obey, but usefulness is tied into obedience," Dr. Ralph Byron of the City of Hope told his Sunday-school class one day when I was visiting. He knew whereof he spoke: he had learned "notable obedience" in the U.S. Marines.

So we thank God because this is the thing to do, as believers. I wouldn't pretend to know how praise and thanksgiving work; I just know they do. I am not one bit analytical about the things that work for me; I'm just thankful for them. What difference would it make if I did understand all about what makes them tick? Would they be more effective? Would praise be more or *less* "conquering" if I could analyze how God makes it work for me? If we were restricted in daily life solely to the use and enjoyment of things we *understand,* what a narrow experience that would be, to say nothing of the advantages we would have to forego.

I don't know how electricity works. But I know it dispels darkness for me; I know it makes the temperature bearable in Southern California these days with our hundred-degree heat; I know it cooks my food and does so many other things that I take for granted. Even though I am totally ignorant of how it works, if the directions say: "Push the button," I push the button. I don't stop to figure out how it will work.

So it is in my personal experience with the response of thanksgiving and praise to God. Seemingly this releases a power beyond our ability to comprehend. It recycles ashes, transforming them into something beautiful; it turns sorrow into gladness; it changes mourning into joy; it gives a "garment of praise for the spirit of heaviness" (*see* Isaiah 61:3). I didn't know anything about this—oh, I knew the verse and where to find it, but I had never personalized and internalized it until I desperately needed what only God could give. So I tried "thanks therapy" and found that it works.

The "garment of praise" fascinated me. A garment is for covering. It helps if it fits, and if it is a color you like. I believe this garment of praise which Isaiah talks about is custom-made for us when we need it. It will never be drab gray; that is the color of "the spirit of heaviness." I think this garment comes just in rainbow colors.

I am afraid that some people who really need it will never have a chance to try on that garment of praise. For at the onset of any and every trial, rather than giving thanks to God, they kick at the circumstance, resent it and resist it, all the while raising their own blood pressure and further compounding their problem.

Admittedly, it is not a natural reaction to praise either God or man when trouble strikes. There has to be something, some strength from above to make this possible. And it is so easy to take the natural route. When we do, we get only what the natural can give us. When we dare to believe God—even against what our senses tell us—believe Him enough to say, "Thank You, God," we get what God can give us.

I repeat that I have no explanation for the alchemy of praise. I just know that I have proved God in some hard situations; I have learned and am still learning to thank Him at such times—and I am learning something of the conquering power of praise. If it has never been your experience to have to lean hard on God, not understanding what is going on, but thanking Him anyway, you cannot know what I am saying. As one of my Scottish countrymen has said, "It's better *felt* than *telt* [told]." *And it's exciting what happens!*

I promised to pray with and for the woman who shared her private trauma with me at the retreat. After we talked for some time, she said that now she felt she could begin to think about thanking God, taking at least one step in that direction. Now I can hardly wait to hear what God is doing for her, for He will meet her more than halfway. When we give thanks, we are doing God's will. When we do His will, we put ourselves in line for His blessing on our lives. No doubt about that!

What is the alternative when we feel we cannot accept, cannot thank God for what comes into our life? Usually we do or say any of half a dozen things:

- *Ask:* "Why me?"
- *Question:* "What did *I* do to deserve this?"
- *Rationalize:* Look around for someone to blame.
- *Complain:* "Why would God do this to me when I'm doing my best to serve Him?"
- *Speculate:* "If there is a God, why did He let this happen to me?"
- *Murmur:* "If God loved me, He would keep this evil from me."

Our questioning so often has a childish petulancy about it, as though God is answerable to us—and not the other way around! I know, for I have asked all the questions. In my case it was more griping than seeking an answer. Not till we come to the place where we do accept and thank God, will we ever find out that it works. This is God recycling us.

For the woman left on her own, the recycling must first be emotional. She must be helped up from the darkness of depression that so often envelops her, before she will be ready to cope with her new life. Those who have lost a mate through death, difficult as this is to bear, have something going for them that the other "widowed" are deprived of—the widow or widower generally is shown sympathy and understanding. Compassionate friends and relatives surround and support them, at least for a time. This is usually not for long enough, however. After a couple of weeks the people who have outdone each other in demonstrating love and caring drop off. It is significant that the period of mourning used to be a year. Is there in this, I wonder, a tacit recognition that it takes this long for the bereaved to recover, to adjust, and to cope with life again?

For the divorced and the deserted there is usually little of either compassion or understanding. Society—and some of the Christian community in particular—is quick to judge and condemn, to fix blame, and slow to help the victims of these tragedies back to emotional well-being and to a place of acceptance in the church and the community. There are, of course, exceptions, people who are warm and loving and accepting and who have constructive help to offer.

It is important that we be extremely careful in counseling a person who is suffering from some emotional trauma. People are grasping for straws at such times and just one thing we say might appear to be the answer, setting them off on a particular course which may not be the best one.

I remember some excellent counsel a friend gave me one time when I needed it. This Christian man said, not once but a number of times, "Jeanette, keep in mind that *God wants to bless you.*" Simple? Of course. Every Christian knows this. We don't even have to think about it. And certainly we don't need someone to remind us of it. Oh, no? What did this "simple" truth say to me? How did it affect my attitudes—perhaps my *future?* Here's how: It said, "Never mind all the contributing factors and the other people involved in what has hurt you. Just believe that God wants to bless you. He will take care of how He's going to do it." And this helped me to shed feelings of self-pity and yes, even bitterness. For this I understood: God is not in the business of blessing a person who would rather dwell on her misfortunes. I did not want to cheat myself of the good things God had in store for me. So I took this good friend's wise counsel, stopped looking backwards, and began to be interested in the possibilities ahead of me as God carried out His program to bless me.

God has always been interested in the widow. The Bible is quite specific about this. (*See* Exodus 22:22; Deuteronomy 10:18; 1 Timothy 5:3–5.) The first-century Christians were mindful of the widows among them and made provision for them; a mark of "pure religion" was caring for the widow (James 1:27).

God is not less mindful of the widowed in our own day.

You *can* thank Him. *Do you dare to try it?*

5

Three to Get Ready

Preparedness is the secret of poise.

Mary Andrews hurried to the bus stop on the corner of her street, but she almost hoped the bus would never come. This was the day she was venturing back into the business world—"I'd rather do anything else," she said to herself.

Like so many other women, Mary had no choice. Her husband had died and she had to find a job in order to survive. That was her reason for exposing herself to what she felt could only be a traumatic experience. It had been so long since she had worked outside the home.

Later that day, in a large business office, two secretaries eyed a newcomer, Eileen, as she approached the coffee machine at break time. "Hmm," the one said to the other, "doesn't *she* look like she knows where she's going!" Between sips of coffee, the other agreed and added, "She certainly has poise, and besides that she looks interesting. Let's go meet her." Two women embarking on the same venture—one admittedly fearful, the other obviously self-assured.

If we could take a peek into Mary's situation and listen in on what her new colleagues were saying about her, we would undoubtedly find what I have learned for myself, that other people accept us on the basis of how they see us accepting ourselves.

Eileen projected a good self-image. Mary (unless, which is unlikely, her attitude toward her self improved between the bus stop and her place of employment) would mirror her own fears about being accepted in the new situation. People would view her as less than confident.

What makes the difference? What would make one person facing a brand-new situation appear assured, and another in the same circumstances shrink from the experience?

One explanation is *readiness.* Nothing is so confidence inspiring as the feeling that we are prepared for whatever is ahead of us. This is true of the student on exam day, the teacher with her daily lesson plan, and the Sunday-school teacher, whether the pupils are kindergarten wigglers, blasé teenagers, or Bible-hungry adults. It is true of the lecturer, the speaker at any function, the minister as he steps into his pulpit. *And it is true of the fifty-plus venturer back into the job marketplace.*

That first icy plunge into a new situation: nobody has shrunk from that more than I have. I can honestly say, "I understand." When we would move to a new church and I had to face all those new people, I sometimes just wished I could run away. Standing at the church door after service, shaking hands, and smiling at everyone: I almost got ulcers. Of course it was unreasonable, for the people were warm and friendly. They would have had a hard time understanding my feelings. It took me a long time to understand them myself. After a while I did. It was a form of pride, I think. I was fearful that people would not like me, that I would fail to measure up to their expectations. Actually I could have saved myself all the fears and just been myself. This is the way to relax other people as well as yourself, and the whole situation eases. No ulcers. People see you as happy with yourself and accept you accordingly.

For the Christian the answer to a good self-image is just appropriating what is already ours. *God* has accepted us. The Bible says so. We are "accepted in the beloved [Jesus Christ]" (*see* Ephesians 1:6). God sees us as worthy persons, as members of His family (John 1:12). We can sing and know the truth of "I'm a part of the family of God." There is no need, then, to be hangdog in our attitude toward ourselves. That goes for the *fifty plus* as well as the *fifty minus.* We can hold up our heads, no matter what the circumstance which throws us into a new situation.

Step One: Appearance

Since first impressions are important, one area in which it really pays to "be prepared" is appearance. People judge by what they see, by another person's looks. So grooming cannot be overlooked. There is something about knowing we look our best that gives a woman (I assume this pertains also to a man) a poise we might not otherwise have. I am not suggesting a great splurge on a wardrobe or spending a week at an expensive spa for health and beauty. I am referring, rather, to taking a critical look at yourself, assessing what could be improved perhaps by a new hairdo, by appropriate dress for the position. It is a good feeling to know that you look just right. Usually this has little to do with natural beauty or the price we pay for clothes. Posture is important. There is something about a person who walks tall and straight which other people admire; usually we turn for a second look. Almost every women's magazine has simple, workable ideas for improving one's appearance. Someone has worked out the procedures and it doesn't hurt to try them.

Diet makes a big difference. Some people are perpetually less vital than they need be, just because they do not eat right. And again this is not necessarily tied to the amount of money we spend for food; it involves making the right choices with the money we budget for food.

Someone has spoken of good grooming as caring enough to look your very best. There is a lot of truth in this, for grooming is mostly just that: caring what you look like. However you achieve it, you cannot overemphasize the importance of a good appearance. It goes a long way toward the poise that makes a good first impression. How you look says a lot about you.

We look better when we are involved in something we really enjoy doing. It shows on the face. So does boredom. Uninvolved people have something missing that makeup can never quite fix. I am not prone to boredom, at least I don't think I am. But I can get pretty worked up over something that is tremendously important to me. For instance, about three-and-a-half years ago I went to the then-new nation of Bangladesh. It was an exciting time preparing for the trip. My son and his wife met me between planes in New York's Kennedy Airport and had attended a dinner the previous evening, at which Dr. Clyde Narramore was the speaker. He and Bruce had chatted about my project and Bruce repeated to me what Dr. Narramore had said, "Bruce, your mother looks ten years younger since she's been planning this trip." And I wouldn't doubt it. There is something so exhilarating about anticipating an exciting experience and then moving into doing it. It makes the blood flow faster—and we look more alive.

So it will pay off if you can view this new step you are about to take as offering you an energizing, stimulating piece of life. It will show in your face.

Step Two: Attitudes

Just as important as appearance in the long haul are our attitudes. No matter how personable an individual looks and how well he or she is at first accepted on the basis of appearance, there is the matter of day in/day out getting along on the job.

Relationships are all-important. In fact, a respected psychologist, Dr. Maurice E. Wagner, states: "What the Bible is all about is *relationships:* one, our relationship with God. 'Thou shalt love the Lord thy God'—(Matthew 22:37, 40)—the first commandment; two, our relationships with other people—'and thy neighbor as thyself'—Christ's second commandment."

What a relaxed atmosphere we would enjoy if the world functioned on this dual-relationship basis. But where most of us live we sometimes have to cope with abrasive people and they have the same problem with us. I remember so well a period of a few months when (every day it seemed) a woman just irked me; she plain rubbed me the wrong way. There was something about her that could rob my day of its calm. Things did not get better even though I thought I was trying. Then one day it dawned on me that this woman was sandpapering my own rough corners. I soon was learning a degree of patience; I was striving to use creative means to win this woman and establish a friendly relationship instead of worrying about what kind of mood I would find her in. I began to thank the Lord for these lessons He was teaching me in getting along with people. At the same time I prayed, "Lord, I don't want to be Your sandpaper to rub the rough spots off other people."

Usually we are the last to see our own faults and idiosyncracies that make us a bit difficult to get along with. The person contemplating a return to the workaday world might profitably take honest inventory of his or her attitudes. If you feel you cannot be objective, you may be fortunate enough to have a real friend who will level with you about little quirks of yours that are annoying. If that is too much to ask of yourself, then why not think about and write down some of the things about other people that irk you. Then face up to the question: "Am I just as guilty of these things myself?"

No preparation you can possibly make will pay the dividends that this self-inventory will, as you begin to work on the different areas in your life. The individual who can get along with other people is always a great asset. It helps when—as part of this preparation—you decide that you will not let other people's behavior control yours; that you will not be simply a reactor. It came as a kind of revelation to me when I learned that I did not have to act according to the behavior of people around me. I do not have to have my temperature set by others; I can choose. This is a good feeling. For example, someone comes along and says something or does something that could easily make me angry. If I do not act too swiftly and return the anger, I am in a position to select my behavior. In this way, nobody is "making me angry."

As in everything that has to do with human behavior, the Bible has a word for us here: "A soft answer turneth away wrath . . ." (Proverbs 15:1).

Also, there's a whole basket of "fruit of the Spirit" that should govern the attitudes and behavior of the Christian, beginning with love, joy, peace, and encompassing patience and gentleness (*see* Galatians 5:22). God has provided us with all the resources we need for good attitudes. And what a world of preparedness that is for the person starting out on a new venture where relationships are so vitally important for any kind of happiness on the job.

Looks good on paper, you may be thinking, *but how do you make it work? It sounds too ideal.* My answer to that has to be that *I* don't make it work; I couldn't. But God can. Believing this, just as regularly as I take my daily vitamins, each morning I turn my day over to God. I find it helps when I am "myself" in my prayer (the Lord knows me anyway). I pray something like this:

Lord, You know all about today. You know my heart and that I could very easily say all the wrong things and likely hurt a person or two. But I don't *have* to, so please help me to be patient and tolerant and kind and loving. People around me know I'm a Christian. Help me not to let them—or You—down today.

What happens when we start the day with God, when we "meet God in the morning, when the day is at its best," as a lovely poem puts it? Actually, the day may seem to go the same way as it does for the person who doesn't pray. The difference is in how I am able to react to what happens. Take the matter of something that provokes me, big or little. On my own I would be a victim of this. Either I would spout off or I would grimly put up with it. With *Christ* empowering me, I can stay calm. This in itself is often half the solution to a problem, for it enables us to retain our capacity to think clearly and creatively. Again I don't have to be a reactor, controlled by what another person does or does not do or say. We talk of the Spirit-controlled life as if it were just the title of a book (which it is) or a high-sounding pious phrase. It is more than that. It is on everybody's level—everybody who has trusted Christ and committed his way to Him. And it works! It is a good attitude-maintainer.

I realize that my assertion that God can make it possible for us to have the right attitudes, to be patient and long-suffering, and so on, may seem just pious talk to you. You may need something more specific, a "how to." Let me say that in my own experience I find this help to be three-pronged:

1. God empowers us by *His Holy Spirit* (John 16:7–15).

2. God strengthens us through *His Word*. In a sense, reading the Bible as our manual for living is no different from reading a manufacturer's manual to find out how best to make a product function. God has made us and He is the final Authority as to how we should be treated and how we should treat other people. And it is all in the Bible.

3. We learn from *other people*. As we observe what works for them, we can adapt the lessons to our particular situations. There is nothing

mysterious about getting along with other people. There *is* a working formula. Jesus gave it to us:

> Therefore all things whatsoever ye would that men should do to you, do ye even so to them. . . .
>
> Matthew 7:12

So simple. So profound. So revolutionizing to relationships.

Step Three: Upgrading Your Skills

There is something about feeling confident that you can really do the work. You may have suffered a severe loss, your ego may even be shattered if it is either divorce or desertion which has made you a "widow." So all the more you will need the sense of competence on the job to bolster you.

Also, methods and machinery change. The supersecretary who has been out of the business field and returns without some kind of updating of her skills may find herself at a loss or somewhat inept with all the new equipment. It is a poor start when you have to be asking about this and that; it makes for less than satisfactory relationships. Not that other people are unkind and inconsiderate; it is just that they are usually busy with their own work. You especially need to consider whether you are using your traumatic problem—whatever caused the bottom to fall out of your world and sent you back into the labor market—as an excuse for not being knowledgeable.

Sometimes I've listened to such conversations as this: "I'm sorry to bother you; I should know how to do this, but you see—" and the person goes into a lengthy sharing of her problem. Few fellow employees want to get caught up in other people's reasons for not being proficient; and they certainly do not want to be expected to carry some of the work load because a newcomer is not up to it.

Respect is important to everyone; self-respect is all-important. It builds one's self-respect when one is ready for the job; other people will also respect the person who is competent through training for the position.

I saw a title which interested me the other day. It was "Bloom Where Your Interests Are." I couldn't help thinking, *How much better to bloom than to wilt!* Upgrading your work skills will permit you to bloom.

Sometimes the training itself can be God's means to open up a whole new future. I know such an instance. A close friend died and left his widow with three children, two well into their teens, and a younger one. Because of long family friendship and because I was not too far away, this new widow clung to me. A few weeks after the funeral I could see her sad state. Her children went off to school, and she just sat there. My heart ached for her. We talked. We prayed together, but all she could see was her life stretching out with loneliness from the time her daughters left in the morning till they returned in late afternoon. Though I am no guidance counselor, no psychologist, I found myself offering her some counsel.

"Have you thought," I asked her, "that it might be good for you to go to business college—or *someplace?*" All I had in mind was to get her out of the house every day, *with a reason for going,* so that she would not wave her children off and then slump into depression for the rest of the day. I had the girls in mind as well as their mother, for the home was beginning to develop an unhealthy gloom. The youngest, an eleven-year-old, particularly tugged at my heart. Her daddy had been her whole world.

So the mother needed to support these children emotionally. There was enough money; that was not her problem. But first she had to find a reason to get up in the morning and face the day—and the future. Because she was basically a well-adjusted person—just crushed by the loss of a very loving husband—she responded to my suggestion. Within a week she had made arrangements, and when her daughters left for school she did, too. It did not take long to prove that this was really God's plan for her at that time. One day a request came for a very specially trained person. Her college work had been in that field. Now with her added business training, she was exactly the person a state agency was looking for; even her years as a minister's wife weighed in her favor for this position. And this is a happy-ending story. She never forgot her husband and the happy years they had together, but God brought another partner into her life. He gave her a new future.

I have sometimes pondered what would have happened to this

woman and her children if she had let one of life's hardest blows knock her out. Instead she recycled. But first she got ready by training for a job.

Undoubtedly a number of other factors enter into the recycling process when life mandates it. But these three basic steps:

- Giving attention to appearance
- Taking an attitude inventory
- Upgrading one's skills

would appear to lead in the right direction for a well-adjusted recycling.

There is security in the familiar: old surroundings, friendly faces, known situations. We cannot, however, expect to go through life without change. And would it be all that interesting anyway? Granted, making a new start has its traumas. But while the cold plunge makes us shiver for the moment, it rewards us afterwards with a feeling of vigor for daring to take it.

Preparation can make all the difference when circumstances force us into a new situation.

6

Realistic Expectations

Work is the means of living, but it is not living

J. G. Holland

Grace and her neighbor down the block met in a supermarket and maneuvered their shopping carts to allow themselves a visit for a minute or two.

"I hear you have a job, Grace," the neighbor said. "That will be something new after such a long time. I'm happy for you," she added with a little pat on Grace's shoulder. "It'll help take your mind off other things."

"That's what I'm hoping," Grace sighed. "At least it won't be so lonely as being around the house all day and—"

Traffic parted the two women and the kindly neighbor called over her shoulder, "Be sure you let me know how things go for you."

Clearly, Grace is a woman who, whatever the reason for her loneliness, is looking to a job to solve her problems. Some people turn to a job in later life out of economic necessity. Others, due to their circumstances, can afford to work on a volunteer basis. Whatever the situation that moves you into the work stream, it is wise to consider what a job can do for you, and what you should *not* expect it to do.

Perhaps the question should be: "Whose needs am I meeting in taking a position?" It always pays to be realistic. Meeting something face on and dealing with it can forestall a lot of problems and difficulties. Let's look first at what a job will *not* do for a person.

A job, no matter how desirable, will not meet all your needs.

Especially, it cannot be expected to meet your emotional needs. Oh, if it is sufficiently demanding of your attention, it will keep you from thinking about your own problems, about how lonely you are, how things used to be, and so on. But no job can cure loneliness or bring back the past. To reenter the working world with such a hope is only to program yourself for disillusionment and disappointment. The person who has such expectations is placing too great a burden both on the employer and fellow workers. People are generally too busy to be sensitive to the point of compensating for a colleague's personal traumas. The newcomer in the office or other place of business who is looking for such treatment may, after a week or so, find herself an object of pity—or people may just not bother with him or her. This would then tend to further any feelings of loneliness and rejection, and the person would blame the job and the people there—when actually one's own unrealistic expectations are at fault. No job will meet our emotional needs, although it *can* be a help in that direction.

There is nothing amiss in having reasonable anticipations as you go back to work. The employer certainly hires a person to meet existing needs, and sometimes this does prove to be a two-way street. Mostly it does not, however, and the greater the employee's emotional need the more unlikely it is that a work situation will meet it. Ultimately, satisfaction has to stem from within, not from our environment. For the Christian, there is the broad-range promise:

> But my God shall supply all your need according to his riches in glory by Christ Jesus.
>
> Philippians 4:19

I have never found an area where God doesn't make good on this promise, when I have trusted Him. Philippians 4:19 is like God's signed blank check to be used whenever needed. As for the job—by all means take it. But expect it to be just that—a job.

There are certain things a job *will* do. Having a job to go to will give you a reason for getting up in the morning, for getting dressed and facing the day. Sometimes when life has dealt us a blow, this is difficult to do, and the longer we put it off the harder it gets.

A job will usually give you contact with people. Whether this proves to be a plus or minus factor depends totally on what you make it. Your own actions (and *re*actions, which are often more telling) can determine how nourishing to your emotions other people will be.

In our relationships with people some things are so simple that they appear to be overlooked. For instance, a *smile* is the finest medium of exchange we have. A smile can dramatically change one's appearance. If you doubt this, try standing in front of your mirror, wearing your "usual" face, and say, "This is what people generally see when they look at me." Then smile at yourself in the mirror. Now what would people see? A light in your eyes, the corners of your mouth turned appealingly up rather than grimly down? And—admit it—you *feel* better when you see the smiling you.

We live in a world where many people are harried and frustrated and tired. Frown lines are carved into so many faces we see. But try smiling at them. (It is important not to wait for the other person to smile first; he or she might be waiting for *you* to smile). A smile is the shortest distance between two people. Not only are you meeting someone else's need for a spot of human warmth, you are meeting your own emotional needs as the other responds. This is something a job will do.

Other simple measures for maintaining good relationships are: being a good listener rather than doing all the talking, appreciating people and telling them you appreciate them by being positive rather than seeing the negative side of everything, and—probably the most important—accepting people as they are and not going about to try to change everyone into a reflection of yourself. When we try to change a person it comes across as: "I don't like you the way you are," or: "You don't quite measure up"—the death knell to a relationship. Having a job gives you a chance to sharpen all your skills at getting along with people. Granted, it is a challenge. But isn't everything in life?

A job will help keep you close to God. You may not have expected a closer relationship with the Lord to be one of the fringe benefits. But it is. For, as Christians out in the bustling business world, often in a dog-eat-dog situation, it takes all the grace of God that we can appropriate to keep us reflecting something of the image of Christ. It is rough some days, to be sure. But Jesus promised, "I am with you always" (*see* Matthew 28:20). *All the days.* The rough days, the testing days, the days when sheer frustration might cause us to quit, or when it would be easier to snap at a colleague than to be Christlike. This is why I say that a job can draw us closer to God. How often, as I have faced a workday, have I prayed:

> Lord, You know how prone I am to get irritated at some people and some situations. [Although God knows all about it, I sometimes mention names in my prayer.] So, will You please give me a special measure of Your love and caring and patience —all I will need today to keep me from being a poor example of a follower of Yours.

And God always comes through. If there is failure, it is on my part.

Another plus of having a job is that it offers opportunities for witnessing. In a non-Christian environment this can be a unique ministry. A few days ago I met a psychiatric nurse who shared with me her experiences as the sole Christian on the staff. "At first," she said, "it was a sheer persecution trip. I couldn't do anything to please the doctors, and I was blamed for things I didn't do. They resented having a Christian in the psychiatric wing. It was real rough." What did she do? Quit? No. "I prayed and reminded the Lord that He had promised to be with me and give me strength," she told me, "and amazingly, things began to change. Now, after a year, I'm one of the most popular people on the staff. And I get so many invitations, and people ask me about my faith. It's just great," she added with enthusiasm.

The lesson would seem to be that a Christian in a secular setting has to work harder and put up with more, in order to earn the respect of the non-Christian. But it is worth it! We can never lose in this venture, for, as God's Word assures us: "Them that honor me I will honor" (*see* 1 Samuel 2:30). It is only as we stick close to God that we can maintain right attitudes and honor God by our speech and behavior.

What are some of the things which hinder our testimony on the job? (For additional material on such attitudes and what to do about them, you may wish to read my book *The Image of Joy.*)

1. A rigid attitude that makes no allowance for differences in people, that does not admit to God's originality in creating us all "different."

2. Having to be "right" all the time, being argumentative to prove you are right (even when it does not make a whit of difference who is right).

3. Demanding perfection of yourself and everyone around you. It is commendable to do good work, of course, but some people make a fetish of it to the point where other people's feelings are unimportant. Here is an area to watch for balance.

4. A closed mind: intolerance of new methods and procedures—incessant references to "how we used to do it." Someone has called this the "skull and crossbones" of creativity.

5. Prejudice—this can be with reference to individuals, to certain customs, food, dress, or almost anything in which there can be a difference of opinion. Prejudice is a particularly obnoxious characteristic because usually it attacks its victim for something the person had nothing to do with and cannot help.

These are just a few. There are other qualities that prevent us from having good relationships with other people. So it is good to take inventory occasionally.

I know of a seventy-five-year-old woman who recaps each day before she settles down for the night. She asks herself, "What wrong things did I do today, and how can I change, to keep from repeating the same wrongs tomorrow? How can I make things better, not only for myself but for other people?"

It may be that you are thinking, *That's all right for this woman, if she's willing to go through with it. But why should I be the one to change?* That is a fair question. But wouldn't your willingness to recognize the need to change, and your efforts to work on it be a mark of your maturity?

I would like to encourage the man or woman who may be fearful about breaking into a new job or returning to work after many years away from this life. Just a few things, such as we have been dealing with, can make all the difference between a bad situation and a happy experience that sends you off eager and excited each morning. It is not necessarily the supertalented person who makes it. Personality goes a long way. Fortunately, personality is not static; as long as we are alive we can change and improve personality-wise.

It is good to keep in mind that there are various abilities which are appreciated (not only those of genius quality):

Availability	The "Here I am" quality
Dependability	Being a person who can be counted on
Responsibility	Being worthy of trust
Accountability	Recognizing a coming day of reckoning and being prepared for it by faithfully discharging one's duty

Each of these "abilities" can be cultivated at any age, and they have little to do with natural endowments. Yet they are in great demand and are much appreciated.

Let me share a personal incident to underscore my point. One day my son, Bruce, said to me, "Mother, I have a backhanded compliment for you. I think you can take it." He explained that he had recently been in a situation where he could not help overhearing a group of editors and publishers talking. Somehow my name came into it, and Bruce heard this: "Jeanette Lockerbie will probably never be a great writer—but she surely is *dependable.*"

Yes, I could take it. In fact, I took it as a compliment and a challenge. After all, how many "greats" are there in a generation! I am happy to settle for being dependable. I understood what the man who made the remark meant. He was saying that, having accepted an assignment, I would follow through and deliver the manuscript on time. (One time I was late because I had broken my wrist.)

Not only are availability, dependability, responsibility, and accountability worthwhile in the job marketplace, they are the very qualities *God* is looking for. Sometimes God has a hard time finding such a person. Remember when He was looking for a man "to stand in the gap" but He found none! (*See* Ezekiel 22:30.)

When we develop these qualities we do ourselves a favor. It builds a healthy ego when we become known as dependable, responsible, and so on. As we are meeting our own needs, we will have all the more to offer on the job. In fact, some people become indispensable because they demonstrate one or more of these abilities.

Above all, concentrate on being a person with the maturity of attitude to turn negative situations into positive ones. This is possible in both family and social situations, as well as in that new venture into the business world.

It will be easier if you set out with realistic expectations.

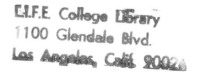

7

How to Grow a Friendship

A friend is one who walks in when the rest of the world walks out.

Author unknown

In the recycling process nothing is more necessary than a friend, a genuine friend on whom we can count. In fact, psychologists are researching whether a person can ever be truly whole without having at least one person to whom he is important. Since this is apparently so meaningful, and since recycling is essentially a bid for renewal and wholeness, should we not seriously think about this matter of friends?

"Good friends are forever. Good friends are for keeps," bleats a radio commercial. Like so many media messages, this one has some surface truth. It would not bear in-depth investigation, however. Otherwise why would we so frequently hear the poignant "We used to be such good friends"?

Actually, friends are like houseplants. They need nurturing. Increasingly we are being told of the miraculous effect of "love" on the ordinary houseplant—how it will respond to the type of caring which goes beyond attention to watering and being in the right exposure for sun or shade.

I am not good at growing plants. Never have been. As a minister's wife I have had all kinds started for me by kind, loving women in the congregation. I would often genuinely admire an African violet, a shiny-leafed begonia, or an exotic gloxinia as I visited in a home. Without fail, I would soon be the recipient of such a plant, and for the poor thing it was almost the kiss of death. Not that the plants quite died. If they had, I could have tossed them out with a clear conscience. But no! They just sat there in their pots, never growing an inch or a new leaf, regardless of how I watered or sunned them and whether it was summer or winter, or New York, Seattle, or California. Climate or geography was not a part of it. The plants brought me neither joy nor pride. *It must be me,* I concluded long ago. I have no green thumb and I know of no way to develop one.

Can it be that some people have a "green thumb" for growing friendships? I was quite old before I ever thought along this line. Growing up, I always had enough friends of the kind that satisfied me. Then, for many years as the preacher's wife, I was surrounded by people who seemed to major in being friendly to me.

As I look back, I wonder how much these friendships cost me— how much I put into them, or if I really valued them. (I think I did, and a number of them have lasted and stood the test of distance.) The day came when there was no eager congregation as part of my life, and I was in a new area in every sense of the word.

Believe me, that was a *recycling* process. And as part of it, I learned about friends and friendship, and that these are all-important for an emotionally balanced life. And friendship is a two-way street. It is reaching out—not waiting to be accepted before offering friendship. (It may be even more difficult for the other person, no matter how shy you feel yourself to be.) I have wondered, *Am I the only person who had to learn this?* Do most people know it instinctively, the way some people have a way with plants?

How did I learn? It was no problem to find congenial acquaintances. If we go where people are, almost surely "like attracts like," and people who have common interests find each other. But I was *busy.* I feel ashamed, even as I write this, at the smugness of my attitude. For all too often the person who excuses herself—on the grounds of being busy—comes across as saying, "It's all right for you to play, but me—I have important things to do." It took more than a few incidents to uncover this truth for me. An invitation to dinner —but I was "too busy." A group spending the day in just plain fun at the beach—but me "waste" a whole day when I could be home writing to help thousands, so that they can have better relationships with other people? Not me! Then one day the sadness on the face of one of this group got to me. She had said, "Let's stop for dinner on the way home, then maybe we can play a game of Scrabble or something at my house. Just a nice evening together." I said I would like to, but I really had to get home. I had an article I was working on and it was near the deadline.

"Oh, all right," she said. But something inside nagged at me that it was not all right. Some time later, this woman remarked, "You just don't have time for your friends, Jeanette, except when it's convenient for you, yourself." Ouch! That hurt. The truth does hurt. But this was truth that brought light. I got the message which was: *Friendship needs nurture.* I have always been grateful that, in spite of her insightful evaluation of my behavior, she still considered me some kind of a friend. She could have said that this was the end of any friendship between us.

Feeding friendships need not be unduly time-consuming to be effective. We can have well-nourished relationships and still pursue our own hobbies. We can contribute to the health of a friendship without neglecting our responsibilities.

Recycling, at any age and whatever the circumstances, will be less painful and less traumatic when we have a few real friends. No one really has, as we sometimes hear it said of a person, "a host of friends." Genuine, true friends, that is. We can have many acquaintances at different levels of emotional involvement, people with whom we are friendly. But it would make little or no difference to them or us were we to drop out of each other's world. And we do not have to feel that we need to work at maintaining such relationships. They are just not that important. Let me add, however, that acquaintanceship *can* grow into a friendship if we feel strongly enough about it to apply the nourishment needed.

I read somewhere that no person is useless while he or she has a friend. In this I see friendship as not for myself alone; I see my friend as having needs that I can meet. This would be a part of "loving at all times." So we need to develop a sensitivity as to what these needs are and what they are not. How often I have heard someone say, "I enjoy my friends, but I wish they would let me have some life of my own." This would be one of the highest forms of friendship: knowing when not to intrude.

One way to improve our friendship quotient is through awareness of what irritates other people, and a determined effort to eradicate any such thing from our own behavior. Mainly it is little things, and a sure way to know what some of these are is to ask ourselves, "What [in a friend's actions or characteristics] irks me; makes me wish she would quit doing it?" Then—question number two: "Am I doing the same thing myself?" If the answer is *yes*—we go to work on ourselves.

Some friendships appear not to need any watering and sunning. You know what I mean—the old friends you may not see or even hear from for months or more. Then you feel like phoning them, or maybe you are in their neighborhood and you just drop in. You do not feel any need for bridges. You can pick up where you left off the last time. "It's just as though we've never been apart"—"Remember when we—" are sure to feature largely in the conversation. These are friendships to treasure, but they are generally very few in number. They survive mainly through memories. They make few demands of us. Yet they come under the category of "forever" friends.

In the recycling process the friend has to "be there." It is important to remember this when we are the friend someone is looking to for support in one of life's difficult turnarounds.

More than anything else, to grow a friendship takes time—and that is something most of us like to hug to ourselves. "It's *my* time," we say (or think). If you are this kind of person, you may want to stop right now—go read something else. Or, and this would be an admirable decision, you may think, *I don't have to be like that. I can learn to become a friend even if it does take my time.* Who wants to be like Napoleon who is reputed to have said, "Ask me for anything but my time." How can we do anything or give to anyone without it costing us time? And what better way to "redeem the time" as the Bible exhorts us (*see* Ephesians 5:16; Colossians 4:5), than to invest it in other people?

Just taking the time for a telephone call says volumes. And it is dreadfully easy to neglect this channel. One thing I have learned and I would like to share with you is: *Do something* about your friendly impulses. *Write* that note. It just takes a few minutes, as we know. *Make* that phone call. I remember so well a particular instance of what I call activating my impulses. It was Saturday morning and I was enjoying doing things around the house—the things that pile up during the week—but I kept thinking of a particular person. It was a persistent thing that I tried to shrug off mentally, but the thought kept recurring. I recall arguing with myself, "You know there are all these things you want to get done this morning and if you stop to phone now—well—" I failed to win the argument somehow. And another thought invaded my mind. *Is it the Holy Spirit urging me to make this call?* I stepped over to the phone. Before I dialed, I investigated in my mind the possibilities of this friend and myself doing something interesting that evening; then with a concrete suggestion to offer I phoned. The voice on the other end was that of a very sick, weak woman, and she was almost pathetically happy for my call.

"How did you know I just needed somebody?" she asked. "I was feeling so bad here all alone."

Believe me, I will always be glad I activated that impulse. Apart from anything I could and did do to help her as a result of the call, the phone call itself was nurture for our friendship, helping it to grow; for caring has to be expressed.

Sadly, some people seem to be able to talk only of the friends they used to have. And they are not referring to persons who have either died or have moved to other parts of the country (distance does not sever friendship, I have found). "Mary [or Joe] and I used to be such good friends"—I have heard this dozens of times. It is true of men as much as women. Usually a world of wistful longing can be read into the voiced words.

What prevents good friends from being "for keeps"?

Sometimes it is neglect such as I was guilty of until I learned what my behavior was doing to my friendships; they could not blossom and they withered for lack of nurturing. One hears in psychological circles these days the contrasting terms *nourishing* and *toxic* as applied to one's own behavior and the effect other people's behavior and attitudes have on us. So it might be wise for you and me to ask ourselves, "Am I a nourishing person, or am I toxic to other people?" Toxic in the sense of being a detriment rather than a positive factor for good.

Sometimes it is a lack of unconditional love. What do I mean by that? Just loving and keeping on loving. Not according to how the other acts or speaks or comes across to you. I would go so far as to say that this is the most important ingredient in any friendship. And

I would be supported in this assertion by many professionals who are discovering the almost limitless benefit that comes to the person who feels and senses this unconditional love toward himself. Said Dr. Donn Moomaw, former football star and now minister of Belair Presbyterian Church in the Los Angeles area, "The most liberating words I have ever heard are 'I have unconditional love for you.'"

Nor did the psychiatrists and psychologists "discover" this great truth. The Bible said it long ago. It is the very essence of what the wise man (Solomon) wrote back in his generation: "A friend loveth at all times . . ." (Proverbs 17:17), or, as the Modern Language Bible (Berkeley) puts it: "A friend is perpetually friendly. . . ." At all times—perpetually. Unconditional love is like that.

At all times? That's what the man said. But think of what that means. When the friend is moody, irritable, petty, selfish, uncommunicative, or when he is talking your head off and you fervently wish he would quit, when he overstays his welcome, when he is critical, whiny, complaining, uncooperative, when he is sick and when he is well. When *you* are feeling like not being anybody's friend. At all times, a friend loves. "How would I rate on that?" I ask myself.

"Forget it," you may be saying. "It would be totally impossible to love someone all the time like that." I would agree with you. Let's face it, the wise man was describing an ideal situation, an ideal friend—and there has only been One in all the history of mankind—*Jesus* is His name. Even the man who wrote this lovely proverb could not have measured up to his own standard. Jesus is the only One who ever could, and He did. He demonstrated unconditional love for all people for all time, in His substitutionary death on Calvary. Then He promised, "I am with you always." All the time.

We cannot make any such promise; nor could we keep it if we did. But we can, human as we are, make a stab at unconditional love. This brand of friendship will forge links which can stand every threat against it. It will take at least the patience of Job. It will mean putting a covering of love over the actions or words of the person we are unconditionally loving. It will mean putting ourselves in another's place, making the same excuses for that person that we do for ourselves. We can usually rationalize our own behavior by "I was tired" —"I was in a hurry"—"I didn't have the right tools"—"I wasn't sure of the way"—and the old standby—"I was too busy."

Unconditional love will think of a good "out" for the friend rather than criticizing or condemning a failing. This attitude of understanding can be the figurative weed killer for the plant of friendship. Unconditional love will always make your friend feel better just because you are there. True friendship has been defined this way: *I love you not only for what you are, but for what I am when I am with you. I love you for that part of me that you bring out.*

Especially in the recycling process, people reach out to the one who will make them feel better about themselves than they are able to without such help. This is because recycling almost always occurs (or the need for it becomes apparent) only when something very worthwhile has gone out of one's life. It can be someone especially loved and needed, or it can be a job that carried esteem-building recognition from other people. Always it is some loss that in his own eyes lessens the one who has sustained it. There is a critical need at such time for a supportive friend to assure some measure of emotional balance.

Sometimes a friendship wilts because of a lack of encouragement. Encouragement is a plant food that nurtures friendship. A quick little word of appreciation—"I'm so *glad* I have you for a friend"—can be the best of soil nutrients (thinking of our plant analogy). And a compliment likewise does wonders. It can be about the friend's dress or hairdo or a piece of handwork or her baking. It is even better when the word *you* is in it. "Any cake you bake is always just right," rather than, "That's a good cake." It should be the *friend* we are building up and nurturing, not a product.

If you are the one who needs a friend to help you through your recycling process, the Bible has another piece of priceless counsel: "A man that hath friends must shew himself friendly . . ." (Proverbs 18:24).

There are some people who complain, "Nobody's friendly to me." When there is truth in the statement it is certainly something to be deplored, especially in church circles where the complaint frequently surfaces. Often, however, the person feeling slighted is a victim of his own attitudes. It may be that efforts to make friends with him dead-end—that he fails to go even half a mile when the other person goes two miles and more to meet him. The nonfriendly person may then draw into his shell and actually glory in being neglected. Or if not glorying, he at least gets some kind of neurotic satisfaction. A psychologist for whom I have a lot of respect submits that loneliness is sometimes a mark of an angry, hostile person. Unwilling to make the slightest move for friendship, he nevertheless gripes that he is left alone. As the Bible says, "I am fearfully and wonderfully made" (*see* Psalms 139:14). Never is this more true than when we begin to analyze our own and other people's behavior.

So if a solid friendship is to be part of the new cycle that will give you a hopeful future, are you going at least partway to meet a friend, to nurture a friendship already begun? As Robert Louis Stevenson observed, "A friend is a present you give yourself."

Another factor that can be disastrous to a friendship is *competition.* The cliché "Two's company, three's a crowd" became overworked because initially there was some truth in the statement. Two *is* company. The third person has a way, very often, of throwing off the balance of a smooth relationship.

I distinctly recall such an occasion. With two friends I started out for a day at the shore. We all liked each other and our lives were sufficiently diverse that we had interesting things to converse about. We had our picnic basket, blanket, sun lotion and everything that should have ensured a relaxed and enjoyable outing. But it didn't turn out that way at all! To this day when it comes up in the conversation between any two of our threesome, no one can agree as to what happened. It just did not work, and I for one learned a lesson that day. Not always do people who get along well with one another have the same measure of rapport when a third comes into the picture. (Have you thought that Jesus sent out His disciples in twos? And Paul wrote: ". . . as much as lieth in you, live peaceably with all men" (Romans 12:18), the inference being that it is not always possible to get along with everybody.)

It is possibly a form of selfishness on the part of one or the other; few of us are really willing to share our best friends. Be that as it may, this competition factor is something to recognize. It cannot always be resolved, so it might be wise not to plan lengthy periods of time with threesomes, unless they have proven workable and have not thrown a monkey wrench into friendships. Sometimes it is better in the long run to be polite but firm, and say you prefer not to be part of a threesome, especially if you have had negative experiences along this line.

In this, I am certainly not suggesting that we put someone down by giving the impression that "I don't want to be with you." By all means we need to go the other mile as Jesus Himself told us, if we would grow friendships. As we pray and seek God's guidance in the matter of friendship, we are taking the one step guaranteed to make us the kind of friend who loves at all times.

8

Will I or Won't I?

There is no more miserable human being than one in whom nothing is habitual but indecision.

William James

"I'm so indecisive. I know I need to make up my mind, but it seems I just can't do it." Does this have a familiar ring?

For many people who are really at a crossroads, who need to recycle, the problem of making a decision is sheer trauma. They recognize that things have changed, that they have to make some kind of move, yet they cannot summon up what it takes to make the decision.

Naturally, it is always easier to tell other people how to do things than to take one's own advice. More than once I have been instrumental in helping a woman who found herself at an impasse and who had to do something which called for a decision. I had a good formula for sorting out one's thinking. You make two lists, a pro and a con, objectively marshalling all the facts. I have done this on a napkin at a restaurant, among other places, as another person grappled with a problem. And if these individuals have been speaking truly (and not just flattering me), this has helped; it has worked for them.

Yes, I had a good formula—until I found it did not work for me! Something was missing when *I* needed to make a major decision. I could not get my logic to click, somehow. I had no sense of "This is it: I can move forward. I've made a good decision."

At the time I was in the fortunate position (as I am now) of being able to discuss and interact with professional counselors, experienced psychologists. I recall about half a dozen lunchtimes when I tossed into the conversation hopper the matter of making a good decision, as a hypothetical question. Doubtless the others thought I was interested from the point of view of writing an article for *Psychology for Living* (which I have edited for a number of years). The discussions were interesting and stimulating, but for the most part they did not go much beyond my own formula. I still had my hang-up. I could not get a clear signal as to what to do in my own situation, and I needed to know. Then—and I will never forget it; it was so simple, yet profound and just what I needed—there was the missing piece in my jigsaw puzzle. Here it is: Use the pro and con method. Settle in your mind that these are the facts *at this time*. Recognize that other, later information might change one or more of these facts. But you *lack* this information at the time you must make your decision. You are deciding on the basis of what *is* today. So go ahead and never look back with an "If I had just waited—"

This one point—deciding on the basis of known factors, then never looking back with nagging regret—came to me like a revelation! One psychologist friend, Dr. Ernest Shellenberg, had hit the nail right on the head, for this had been a problem. "What if—!" Every decision of any significance had found me later deploring that I had not decided differently. This, in spite of the high-sounding phrase I had handed out with my pro-and-con-list counsel. "History does not reveal its alternatives," I had told each one. (Which is interpreted as: "You'll never know what might have happened if you had chosen other than you did.")

The new insight really liberated me from my indecisive fears. Yes, I have sometimes looked back and seen how things might have turned out differently if I had taken another course. But when I know that I have decided on the basis of all the *known* facts, this has produced a beautiful peace of mind.

Some people are obsessed with "What if I make the wrong decision!" Has it occurred to you that if we are not courageous enough to decide and then make our move, we may lose out on a piece of God's good plan for us?

Another important point to consider is that it is never wise to try to make a decision while you are too close in time to a traumatic experience. You are still too emotionally involved to be objective. Given a little time, your perspective will change and your decision will have a sounder basis. God's purpose will begin to become evident. In the seeming evil, God's goodness will begin to shine through. The day came when the shamefully treated Joseph was able to say to those who had so mistreated him, ". . . ye thought evil against me: but God meant it unto good . . ." (Genesis 50:20). We cannot—ever—know what tomorrow will bring.

Since we cannot know what a day will bring forth, I am inclined to agree with something I heard Senator Alan Cranston say on the radio some time back: "Make your decision. Don't agonize over it. Even if it's not the best decision, we learn through making wrong decisions."

When we have a decision hanging over our heads—when we are living with a big "if"—it is difficult to be effective in the daily business of living. We are just not at our best. Also, the waiting and the dillydallying has in it a sense that "I'll be wiser tomorrow than I am today; by putting it off, I will guarantee that my decision will be foolproof, perfect, and never to be regretted." In our hearts we know this is not so, yet we let ourselves be plagued by this superirritant: *indecision.*

God can give us His guidance just as perfectly today as He will tomorrow. It is now my strong belief that if we want first the will of God in our lives, the Lord will cause us to think straight in this matter of decision. What we do not know, God *does* know. And the Bible says, "If any of you lack wisdom, let him ask of God . . . and it shall be given him" (James 1:5).

God has promised:

I will instruct thee and teach thee in the way which thou shalt go: I will guide thee with mine eye.

Psalms 32:8

How does God guide *us?* Because we are all different, and our circumstances differ, our creative God works in guiding us in the way that is best for us. He has no prepackaged guidance kits marked A, B, or C—nor does he guide us on the basis of averages or "what recent surveys show." To our God you and I are not statistical averages. We are individuals with differing situations in life.

I have heard Bible teachers define *guidance* in a number of helpful ways, and from the sum of it and from my own experiences with God, I have formulated my own three points which I will share with you.

1. *God guides through His Word.* The leading of God will never be contrary to the *teaching* of His Word. Be wary of supposed "guidance" which violates this principle. Since most of us are not Bible experts, if you are in doubt on this first point, I would suggest you consult with someone, perhaps your pastor, who is knowledgeable about the Bible and whose judgment you trust. There are occasions when, indisputably, a verse has seemed to leap from the pages of the Bible and the exact piece of counsel is there. In a practical sense at such times: "Thy word is a lamp unto my feet, and a light unto my path" (Psalms 119:105).

2. *God guides through circumstances.* For the most part God works naturally. I generally find that He uses other people as He meshes the "all things to make them work together for our good" (*see* Romans 8:28). However, God *is* God, the God of miracles. Significantly, even as I am writing this, a Dino recording on my phonograph is telling me that "It is no secret what God can do." And it really isn't! God is not locked into any method we can dream up or which we have observed in His dealings with others close to us. I have to remind myself of this at times. When a problem arises I have sometimes found myself spelling it out to God in my prayer and then suggesting a way in which He could solve it. God does not slap my fingers or say, "That's *My* department," but I am glad that I usually realize it is His department—and He can and does handle it. So look for God's hand in the circumstances affecting your decision.

3. *God guides through an inner voice.* There is a peace, an assurance that comes when you have sought God's help in the decision that has to be made, when, in line with His Word, circumstances have combined to make you feel: "This is the way; walk ye in it" (*see* Isaiah 30:21).

The proof of this inner peace is that you cannot be talked out of it. This I know to be true. Some years ago I had the sole responsibility of making a major decision about buying a house. My husband was a thousand miles away fulfilling speaking engagements, and it was an emergency situation in the postwar years when housing was at a premium. Through the help of the Lord and my oldest brother, the "right" place was located. I "knew" it was for us. Financially it was beyond our resources, yet, even with my inbred Scottish caution, I felt the Lord was in this matter. Meanwhile, my dear brother John (whose advice I would never scorn, because he is wise and because I know he loves me and wants the best for me) had some reservations. I can still hear his words as I insisted that I felt in my bones that this was God's will: "God is not committed to perform what you think is His will."

I will never forget this gem of insight, given as it was with a spirit of cooperation and love, not as any kind of put-down to my faith. God honored the faith which was, after all, His gift—I cannot manufacture faith. I never doubted in this instance. I did ask the Lord for a sign and He graciously gave it. What I am saying in sharing this incident is this: When the inner voice is God's voice, not even those dearest to you can convince you otherwise, however pure their intent. The inner peace is past other people's understanding; it is between God and you to meet your special need.

A story is told of the famous preacher F. B. Meyer when he was crossing the English Channel. The pilot had come aboard and the minister was up on the bridge with him. "How do you know when you are safely on course in this dangerous channel?" Mr. Meyer asked the pilot.

"See yonder three lights?" and the pilot indicated them. "When they become one, then I know I'm right on course."

"Even so," Mr. Meyer would tell his congregation, "when the Word of God and conditions in my own life and the peace of God in my heart are as one—when they line up like the three lights in the channel becoming one—then I know I am on God's course for me."

Once we know we are "on course," it is a mark of maturity to be able to make the decision that has to be made and then live with the consequences of it. We do not look for such maturity in a child. In fact we can expect to see a normal youngster be hard put to make up his mind as to which toy or which candy bar to choose when a whole array is before him. (We should, of course, encourage children to make decisions whenever suitable, so that they learn that the results are to be lived with.)

God is a wise and a loving Father. He will and He does guide us. But He loves us too well to make our decisions for us. He would violate His own principle of Creation, were He to do this. For one of the glories of being a human is this very privilege of choice. Risky as it was, God gave us a free will. He lets us make the decisions.

You can decide whether used cans and old bottles will be recycled —or tossed into the trash can. These objects have no say in the matter. You, the owner, have the sole prerogative as to whether these inanimate things will have a future. By right of Creation and by the double right of redemption, God owns us. But yet He yields to us the right to make our own decisions.

If today you find yourself in the position of being plagued by the demon *indecision* and you know you must decide, why not try these workable steps. Just doing something, rather than sweating it out in your mind, will help clarify your thinking.

I. List the *options* open to you: moving to another place, seeking a job, going back to school, inviting someone to live with you to share expenses, and so on.

2. Under each option, set down the good things and the negative —the *pluses and minuses* of such a course of action. You might wish to list them under such headings as IF I DO and IF I DON'T, since *IF* is such a major part of your considerations. Be as objective as you possibly can. Refuse to be swayed by indefinite aspects of the situations.

3. Say to yourself aloud, "I realize that some of these determining factors could change. But I am making my decision on the basis of what *is*, what I know *today*, not on what I do not know about the future."

God gave us a mind to reason with, in order to have it move on our will. The ability to make up your mind starts with the *will* to do it. In turn, this ability to make a good decision increases your self-confidence, gives you a rare sense of accomplishment—a sort of "I did it!" Usually other people will also have added respect for you.

So—make your decision. Move ahead on the basis of it, and welcome the experience of recycling. March up to it with your head high, as though it were a door marked OPPORTUNITY—*with your name on it!*

9

Steer Clear of the Negative Crowd

It is almost fatal to an idea to share it with the perennially negative person.

There is one thing that people and the weather have in common: they affect other people.

Mary could hardly wait to share her good news with someone who would listen. She had been trying for weeks to find something that would give meaning to her days, make it worthwhile getting up in the morning. Now one avenue she had investigated had opened up for her. She picked up the phone and eagerly called a friend. The friend listened—between questions and side remarks she was making. Then she said, "Stop a minute, Mary! You're so steamed up over this opportunity, but have you thought how much of your time it's going to take? Have you considered how it will tie you down? And, anyway, are you sure it's the kind of thing you want to do? I'd be careful before I committed myself if I were you!"

The two women talked a little more, then Mary put a halt to what would have been a lengthy admonition. "All right, Susan, I'll think about what you've said," and she hung up the receiver. The light had gone out of her face, the excitement from her eyes. Somewhat wearily, she slumped into a nearby chair; doubts crept into her mind. *Should she forget the whole thing?*

Just a telephone conversation. But the person on the other end had effectively stolen all the joy the day had promised. Suppose Mary had called a different person and her news had been met with: "That's just great, Mary. I'm so happy for you. This is just what you've been needing in your life. Of course you know it will take a lot of time. But I'm sure you've given thought to that." This is positive feedback which reinforces—as against negativism which deflates and discourages. The positive is the sun beaming forth, the negative is gloomy, heavy clouds.

It never pays to surround ourselves with people who have negative dispositions. It is wise to talk things over with someone else when we are about to make a move which will affect our lives and our future, for it is usually true that two heads are better than one. Talking things over clarifies our own thinking, in addition to whatever help we receive from the other person's viewpoint and evaluation. But nobody needs the counsel of someone who can see only the gloomy side of things. Some people seem to major in sticking pins in other people's balloons.

I am often amazed at how one person can affect another. Take this situation: Joe, newly retired, is doing volunteer work for a charitable organization. He is beginning to feel dissatisfied with certain things and during a coffee break ventilates some of his feelings. Someone sitting near him chips in: "Oh, but Joe, think of some of the *good* things!" and he begins to enumerate them. Joe listens and you can almost see the muscles of his face relax. He had been edging away, but now he sits down, pulls his chair closer, and within minutes is engaged in wholesome discussion of his responsibilities.

A brief conversation—but it changes a man's outlook.

To some degree we are all guilty of this negativism at one time or another. Confession is good for the soul, so let me share an incident with you.

I had actually been in the process of taping my thoughts on this matter of being positive or negative in our effect on other people when I arrived at my office at the same time as one of the psychologists. We parked alongside each other, and as I eased out of my Datsun, I began, "Seems I get later every day, Zel—can't seem to get going in the morning—caught a bug when I was in New York at Christmas and it just hangs on—"

Suddenly the incongruity of it dawned on me. Here I had been preparing material to help people to be positive, and to surround themselves with positive people and—*I did it again!* It did not matter that listening to people's problems was this man's profession. That never occurred to me. He is a colleague and I was spouting off, being about as negative as anyone could be. Why were not my first thoughts as I greeted a person in the morning something pleasant, something positive to remember through the day? Zel Brooks will remember, for we both had a good laugh when I told him the irony of the situation. "And you'll make this book, Zel," I assured him.

I am not usually such a gloom spreader. In fact, my response to the inane "How are you, Jeanette?" is the equally meaningless "Fine, thank you," to which I generally add, however, "Isn't that the *only* way to be?"

It is almost fatal to an idea to share it with the perennially negative person. The response will go something like this: "Oh, that's nothing new. I know somebody who tried it and it didn't work." Or: "It may look all right at first, but just be sure there isn't a catch in it."

If we realize that this kind of thinking is as fixed as a footprint in cement, and that no matter what the conditions this person will see the gloomy side, then we are not so likely to be swayed by such an opinion. Even so, such a lack of enthusiasm tends to dull the luster of what had till then seemed bright and exciting. There is something about us that needs the reinforcement of someone else's opinion. This is especially true when life's circumstances cause us to recycle. Therefore, when our enthusiasm is met with scepticism, with pessimism and negativism, it creates sinking feelings. We may easily begin to have doubts—about not only the new venture but ourselves and our ability to "make it."

In the same way as we should avoid deliberately taking toxic food or medication, we need to—for our emotional well-being—avoid too much association with "toxic" individuals.

Like so many emotional hang-ups, being perpetually negative may be a bid for attention. The person may have been cheated in childhood of the satisfaction of his basic emotional needs and is still trying to compensate, as an adult. I do not buy the whole package of some psychologists and psychiatrists who would have everything in our behavior stem from our parents ' attitudes towards us. I believe firmly that there comes a point at which each of us is responsible for his or her own behavior. Nevertheless, we are to a degree what our parents programmed into us. It is difficult to throw off old patterns. The person who was surrounded in youth by pessimists, by negative-thinking adults, has been bent that way, and change comes slowly.

What happens when we are surrounded by such people? Let's go through just one typical morning. You step out of your house and a neighbor says, "Looks like rain." Nothing in that statement, by itself, to affect you unless you had planned your day around the expectation of no rain.

Farther down the block another neighbor greets you and then remarks, "Are you feeling all right? I've seen you looking better."

You go on your way to the supermarket. At the meat counter a customer turns to you with this query: "Do you suppose this meat is fresh?" or the complaint: "I don't think you can trust these scales," or some other evidence of distrust and dissatisfaction.

You have to catch a bus to go to another part of town. Standing at the bus stop with you is a frowning person griping, "These buses! They're never on time; don't know why they have schedules."

You arrive at a department store where you had ordered an item that was to be ready for you that day. But it isn't there. You feel a sense of irritation more than the slight inconvenience calls for.

On the way home, walking the block from the bus stop, you see the mailman heading up the street. "I don't suppose he'll have anything for me," you say to yourself, "or if he does, it won't be anything worthwhile."

The rest of the day begins to stretch out with no bright spots in front of you. Then—like a flash—you catch yourself. And just in time—before you sink into a morass of your own making.

What has happened? You have been surrounded by gloomy, pessimistic people until your own thinking has begun to warp. At this point the healthy thing to do is ask yourself, "Is this my own thinking, or has all the negativism of those other people rubbed off on me?"

Everybody has to live with certain frustrations. That is part of being a member of the human race. The average well-adjusted person recognizes that life *does* have its built-in potential for problems and irksome areas. Thus he is not thrown by every little wave that makes ripples; he saves his reactions for the important things that call for response. Even then he deals in specifics and does not harangue about "everything being wrong, everybody being unfair," and such generalizations. The congenitally negative person, in contrast, is almost always less than logical, and rarely deals in specifics.

As Christians, we should be the most positive of people.

- We have been positively born again (1 Peter 1:3).
- We have positive forgiveness (Ephesians 1:7).
- God has made positive promises to us (2 Peter 1:4).
- We have a positive destination (John 14:1–4).

What then should cause us to have negative feelings? (Negatives are all right in the photography business; but in the business of life, we can opt for *positives.*) There are times, however, when we have to take a negative stand. This is something different from being a person of negative temperament. On the issues of sin and godlessness we need to sound out, "No! I am against it." In fact, we need to take a *positive* stand against these negatives: drugs, alcohol, personal immorality, all forms of evil which destroy people. We also need to stand against everything else that God is against, that violates His commands. But this is not the negativism we are concerned with in this chapter. Rather, we seek to minimize the pervading spirit that sees only the dark side of everything and, because gloom is contagious, inflicts itself on other people, contaminating everyone it contacts.

Another brand of negativism is that found in certain Christians who seem to pride themselves on what they *don't* do. Just a day or so ago I was with a young woman who has not been a Christian very long. She said, telling me of her earliest experiences with Christians, "I thought, *There's an awful lot of don'ts in this religion.*" She is a happy, zealous person and the *don'ts* did not affect her adversely, because she was won to Christ through an extremely loving Christian —and not till later did she learn of the particular mores and taboos held by some Christians.

It has been my experience that the world is singularly unimpressed with what we don't do—with our negatives.

Have you ever asked a person, "What is a Christian?" and received this reply: "A Christian is a person who doesn't drink, doesn't smoke, doesn't play cards, and doesn't go to the movies"?

I'm not making pronouncements on any or all of these forms of behavior. I would say, however, that this list is not a description of what a Christian is. A Christian is one who follows Christ, who has accepted Him as Saviour and Lord of his life, and who strives to live to please Christ. Christ was no isolationist. Nor did He insulate Himself against the world in which He lived. Just the opposite. He "dwelt among us," the Bible tells us (*see* John 1:14). And one of the accusations against Him by His enemies was: "He eats with publicans and sinners" (*see* Matthew 9:11).

We have been stressing that, for our own emotional well-being, we should stay away from the chronic pessimists. But you may be saying, "Are we not supposed to help people? Would it then not be better to spend time with them and try to help them out of their dilemmas?"

I can only ask if you have *tried* doing this. If so, what has been the response? Rarely is the negative-oriented person, even when he is a Christian, very receptive or amenable to suggestions that he be more positive in his approach to life. You may be told in no uncertain terms that it is you who are out of touch with reality, that you either do not care what happens to our world, or that you are just not in possession of the facts. Such people even appear to resent that we are not negative in our outlook. They do not want our sunshine; they like their own gloom. There seems to be some strange kind of gratification for them in this. They can manage to be unhappy even when there is nothing to be unhappy about.

We certainly need to be tolerant, not judgmental in our attitude. When we are condemning, we give the person even more reason and justification for his feelings. We can never know what has made the person develop in the way he has, and should pray for him—feeling, *There but for God's goodness go I.* To keep ourselves on an even keel, however, we need to associate for the most part with well-adjusted, positive-thinking people.

It would be good if simply being positive ourselves would cause people to become less negative in their outlook, but they seem to have such a large compartment in which they store all the "bad" things that have ever happened to them or to others they know. And their memory for people and things, which in their opinion have caused unpleasantness, is right at the front of their brain. These are the memories which immediately surface when *we* try the positive approach with the negative thinkers. They have a very small store of good things on which to call.

We do people a favor when we look on the bright side, when we see the doughnut rather than the hole, the rainbow rather than the rain. We also do ourselves a lifelong favor.

By all means we should try to reverse the negativism trend in ourselves and in others, as they will let us help. Unless we and they deal with this problem we are in for a miserable old age. Aging has too many strikes against it already, without our deliberately approaching it with pessimism and gloom.

God's promise to His people is particularly encouraging for those who are fifty plus: "They shall still bring forth fruit in old age . . ." (Psalms 92:14). Before recycling into fruit bearing, some of us may have to first recycle our attitudes from negative to positive. It is never too late to start!

We will do all the better if we surround ourselves with positive people, steering clear of the negative crowd. When we do have to be with them, let's make up our minds ahead of time that we will not let them control our thinking.

There will always be someone around to throw cold water on an idea. All the more, then, do I appreciate Elisabeth Elliot's maxim: ". . . it is our business to find out what we're good at and then, if it is not inimical to God's order, *to do it* [italics mine]."

10

Where the Opportunities Are

I think of opportunities
That I allowed to die,
And those I took advantage of
Before they passed me by.

James J. Metcalfe

At a family conference the discussion centered on programs for Senior Citizens. Later a couple in their thirties were discussing their parents, in the light of what they had just heard.

"Can you see Mom taking advantage of any of those good suggestions?" the man asked his wife.

"No, I really can't," she answered, "and it makes me kind of sad. I would so much like to see her happy. Mom's problem is that she sees herself as sort of in the past. She just isn't open to suggestions of what she might do now that she has more time than she's ever had. We must be patient with her, but try to get her out of herself," the daughter-in-law concluded.

"Maybe if we take some of these brochures and stuff and just leave them with her, she will read them and—who knows!" the son said with a note of optimism. "After all, she's only in her fifties."

This concerned younger couple were well advised in their decision to make valuable information available to the fifty-plus mother. Generally, motivation and inspiration are based on information.

One of the great opportunities for the fifty-plus person is to return to school or college. Most of this age group were young people during the depression, and college was out of the question for many of them. Now, however, there is a tremendous emphasis on adult education. I often hear radio announcements encouraging people to sign up for classes held at almost any hour—morning, afternoon, and evening sessions are offered. Usually the fee is just a few dollars, and some courses are free. And many can lead to a new future.

What an opportunity to activate a dream!

Just this morning a gray-haired employee, working part-time in his retirement, said to me, "I'm studying Spanish." I really admire such a person. He is not only opening a channel of communication in a locality where Spanish is a second language, but is also keeping his mind alert.

Some of the people I meet in my research really amaze me. One woman shared that she had obtained her first driver's license in her fifties and that she had just earned her first college credits in psychology and electronics. ("I got *B*s," she said.) She works part-time in an office and does not neglect her husband or her home. Her hobbies are music, books, and "my neighbors' children." She says, "No, I'm not brilliant or big and strong. But I do have a lot of drive and I'm connected to the God who made the atom and the electron! He has given me so much to live for."

Increasingly we hear of persons who have developed their latent talents, surprising themselves as well as other people. "Empty days are nothing but poor imagination," said Jane Gunther, widow of the author of the *Inside . . .* books.

Taking advantage of opportunities, or—this takes more initiative: *making* opportunities—can truly be called "retirement into fulfillment." This phrase was coined for me in an interview with a couple who have done just that, retired into a life of total fulfillment.

This couple, successful farmers in Michigan, had been urged, as have many others in the middle years, to take it easy. "Retire to the Florida sunshine and enjoy life. You've worked long enough." They were fifty plus, but not ready for retirement. All their lives they had been busy in their local church, in the community, and working with the Gideons International, and the Christian Businessmen's Committee. Looking back, they now see their work and interests as preparation for their retirement years.

A fire on their farm property made them realize how quickly temporal things lose their value, a reminder of the words of Christ in Matthew 6:20 about laying up "treasures in heaven" where they can not be devalued by moth, rust, theft (or fire). They began to make intelligent investigation of the needs of various Christian organizations for such services as they themselves could offer. They narrowed their search and ultimately found God's place for them—in California. For some five years they have made themselves almost indispensable with their varied talents and skills and unfailing cheerful willingness. I know, for I have been alongside them in one organization during these years.

"By giving of ourselves we receive a greater blessing than by merely contributing of our finances," they have discovered. "Then we have the great satisfaction of working as part of a team and accomplishing things that we individually could not do. We don't need rewards, but they come in the form of warm, wonderful response from people in whom we've shown interest and concern."

This couple's advice to others nearing retirement would be: "Plan to spend your time for other people instead of relaxing in a rocking chair. Take some training to prepare yourself for service where God can use you in your retirement years. Then, like us, you will realize that retirement can be the harvest time of life."

This couple would be joined in their retirement philosophy by the founder of the American Association of Retired Persons and the National Retired Teachers Association, Ethel Percy Andrus, who wrote:

> We are in great measure the architects of our added years. It may not be in our power to arrange for ourselves good living quarters, a decent wage, but it is within our power to enrich our later years by maintaining wholesome personal contacts with our fellows and by using our leisure time in some useful activity.

One of the secrets of "maintaining wholesome personal contacts" is not being afraid of new experiences. I keep hearing of people in the fifties and older who are launching out on new seas. One woman in our area, feeling bored and somewhat useless, responded to a plea from the Red Cross Transportation Unit. She began to provide transportation for the blind and for crippled children. She delivered blood to the hospitals and blood donors to the blood banks. Her "temporary" involvement has lasted eleven years—fulfilling, need-meeting years.

There is great satisfaction in reaching out and giving what is the most important commodity anyone has: our time. I remember some years ago hearing repeated radio announcements appealing for volunteers in our local hospital. I had some time, I thought, so I called and offered a few hours each week. It developed that the real need was for Saturday evening and Sunday afternoon; these were the times when volunteers had other plans. So throughout one winter I did my stint as a Pink Lady. (No hardship; I like pink.) My chief duty, since it was during visitors' hours, was monitoring the visitors:

"No more than two at a time, please."

"Sorry, this patient is not permitted visitors. Doctor's orders."

"Oh, too bad you didn't know your friend was discharged today."

I kept careful account of the visitor cards and in the process probably became a little unpopular with a few people. But usually, when a prohibition is accompanied with a smile, people are reasonable rather than belligerent. Between times I had the pleasure of delivering flowers as they arrived for a patient, always a rewarding chore. Other volunteers wrote letters for patients, read to them, distributed library books, and manned the notions and candy cart.

I doubt that there is any hospital that would not welcome help in these and other areas which its own staff cannot possibly manage in these days of general understaffing. Usually a call to the hospital will be referred to the person in charge of volunteer work.

It is a good feeling to get involved with people and to help meet their needs. In my two-hour stints I was witness to both life and death —to the extremes of human emotions: the heights of joy when a patient recovered, and the depths of despair over those who did not. Nothing will minimize our own real or imagined ills as being with people who are sick and suffering. Each time I left with a renewed sense of gratitude to God for His goodness and mercy in graciously giving me a healthy body and a sound mind.

Opportunity taking is not, however, restricted to the healthy. How many are the instances of people who are overcoming physical handicaps and accomplishing things that leave the rest of us amazed!

Mrs. Williams, a fifty-five-year-old from Florida, is an example. Her stated aim in life is "to put as many Gospels into as many hands in as many lands" as she possibly can. But ten years ago this woman suffered a stroke that paralyzed her left side. Nevertheless, in 1972 and again in 1975, she made trips that took her to New York, Copenhagen, Athens, Zürich, Cairo, Beirut, Ammān, Damascus, and Israel. On the second trip she distributed over two thousand pieces of Christian literature.

"I can walk a little with a leg brace and a quad cane [sometimes called a walker], but for any distance I need my wheelchair and the help of friends," Mrs. Williams tells me.

Biblical history fascinates her, and while she cannot always go where others from the tour bus walk for sightseeing, she makes good use of the time. Local people surround her and eagerly accept the literature she has for them. In Jordan she found a young Bedouin who spoke English, so she persuaded him to be a missionary and share the teaching she gave him with others living in caves nearby. Before the bus pulled away she had the joy of hearing him loudly repeating the words on the tracts she had given him.

In giving me permission to share her story, this dauntless lady wrote, "I believe this may encourage others who have problems to get busy in some way for God—then watch their own troubles diminish. I'd like to urge Senior Citizens (even with strokes) not to give up. These ten years I've found I can do just about anything I've ever done, except climb a ladder or steps if there isn't a handrail."

She does her own housework and has a mailing ministry in about fifteen countries. Besides, she contacts new people who move into her area, and services literature racks in a number of public places with Gospel material.

It goes without saying that most people, no matter how willing they are, will not have such an exotic ministry. They will find their opportunities nearer home, but they will not be less important if they are meeting a need, reaching out with their time and skills and concern for other people.

A key factor in the opportunity business is *motivation,* which is a whole area of life in itself. Not long ago I met a woman who had been challenged to get involved in a certain worthy cause. Her response? "Why should I? I have my own problems."

Does there have to be a "should" to get us going where there is a need we can meet? Some people have a low level of motivation, and since we are all different, we should not judge each other in this respect.

Some have never seriously thought of such considerations as:

- Life is for living—not for sitting on the sidelines.
- God will hold us accountable one day for how we lived *at every age* and, yes, even when life has dealt us a blow, for that can be a part of our growing and maturing.
- Living life to the full generally keeps a person younger in heart and in spirit and, many times, in appearance. In our youth-culture society that should be worth some points.
- The person who questions, "Why should I?" is in effect saying, "What's in it for me?"

For those who need this special bit of motivation, let us consider what *is* in it. One thing that cannot be discounted is that when we can forget our own problems, get up from the depression couch, and look around for a place to help, we gain the benefits of virtually becoming once more a member of the human race. I recall in my own experience a time when I felt that all I wanted to do was just stay home and not have to be responsible for being alive and functioning from nine to five —five days a week. If I could just stay by myself and write, I would be happier. But my daughter-in-law, Lory, bless her, cared enough to discuss this with me in a letter, after I had aired my views:

> My thought on this, Mom, is: just don't cut yourself off from people who give you the vitality that you obviously have. We all need that day-to-day contact that helps to keep us productive and people-oriented instead of self-centered. I know you know what I mean, Mom.

I did know. And I listened and heeded. My daughter-in-law was so right. Other people's vitality rubs off on us, and ours on them. I have been so grateful for my Lory's insight and loving concern that she cared enough to express.

It may cost you some effort, some arousing, for you to take advantage of opportunities. But it will pay off every time. It is always exciting to see how one opportunity leads to another: how life pivots at times on the seemingly smallest circumstance. It makes every day a fascinating possibility. My own experiences have convinced me of this. Let me share an example with you. We might call it "The Case of the Missed Assignment."

It was the annual Christian Writers Conference held at Wheaton, and I had a spot on the program (after some years of being an eager soaker-upper at this fine conference). Don Crawford was an editor who was looking for me, and we got together. He took me along to Tyndale House Publishers and did an interview on my world travels and my writing to that point. Then he revealed his purpose, asking if I would do some like interviews for *Christian Times,* with West Coast people. That day Don gave me a sheet on a California woman who seemed to have all the makings of a good story. I went on my way, enthusiastic about this first assignment for *Christian Times.* On my return home I set out to interview the woman in Glendale.

Driving along Colorado Boulevard in Glendale, I spotted a parking place (a kind of phenomenon at that time of day) right in front of Gospel Light Publishing. How little are the things that often shape our lives! It made sense to stop, for I was then working on an article for them, and it was better to talk it over in person than on the telephone. While I sat in that editor's office, a door opened into my future. The executive editor, Lois Curley, had learned that I was in the building, and called to say, "Don't let Jeanette go." She then sent a secretary to escort me to her office. There she told me of their need for a book by Dr. Clyde Narramore, and that Dr. Narramore could not accomodate them at that time. However, he had given his permission for a writer to do the book they wanted, if Gospel Light could find a person who knew something of his field and *who could write.* (He was most sceptical about the latter.) He had qualified his "I don't know such a person and I don't think you will find one" with this: "I do know one person who could do this book"—and he named me. Apparently he had been reading some of my material from time to time. He was further discouraging, however, when he said, "But you won't get Mrs. Lockerbie; she's now living in New York."

"And here you are!" Lois was no more surprised at seeing me than I was at hearing her request that I do this Narramore book. "Take Dr. Narramore's pearls and put them on your own string!" is the way she put it.

At first I demurred, "I can't do this kind of stuff," but by the time I had been fed everything Dr. Narramore had ever written, I was hooked on Christian psychology. So in my condominium at Huntington Beach, I alternately read and swam for six weeks that summer while working on *How to Succeed in Family Living* and following it with a Teacher's Guide with the same title.

At one point I asked Lois to set up an appointment for me with Dr. Narramore. He graciously escorted me over the lovely grounds of the Narramore Christian Foundation and introduced me to the staff. Then, back in his office, he invited me to join his staff as writer, and editor of *Psychology for Living.* Some months later I accepted the position, and year by year it has been a stimulating, growing experience.

The assignment for *Christian Times?* I never did find the woman I was to have interviewed, although subsequently I did a number of such interviews for my editor friend. But as time has proven, this was God's turnaround time for me. I switched from free-lancing—sort of "playing" at writing as a hobby—to a career the Lord knew I would need for personal fulfillment and ultimately to make a living. Some eight and a half years and nine books later, the events are as clear in my mind as they were on that spring day in Glendale when I missed an assignment.

Generally, opportunities do not come looking for us, or if they do, it is likely we will find that "opportunities knock but once." I have never ceased thanking God for leading me to walk in when He opened that door.

I would suggest to anyone really interested in recycling, for whatever reason, that you pray that God will lead you to the *right place,* at the *right time,* with the *right combination of people.* I believe this is a good prayer and acceptable to God. It might just amaze you, as it has me a number of times, how God will arrange things. And when *He* does the bringing together, you can be sure the outcome is in His will. This is the happy place to be, I have found.

"How will I know it is God's doing?" you may be questioning. This is a valid question, and I'm no oracle, but I would interpret—as God's doing—anything that cannot be explained in any other way and that does not violate God's principles. You may be able right at this moment to turn a leaf in your memory book and recall an instance that was unmistakably God's doing in your own life. And God is the same—yesterday, today, and forever.

Where are the opportunities? Many of them are all around us. As far as the usual run of paying jobs is concerned, people have access to local agencies. There are special part-time opportunities for members of the Association of Retired Persons (and a similar organization for retired teachers). This agency maintains such a service.

If part-time work interests you, you will be interested in a bill currently before the Senate. If it becomes law, the federal government will create a wealth of part-time opportunities at all but the very highest levels of government.

The proposed Part-Time Career Opportunity Act defines part-time work as sixteen to thirty hours per week. In introducing the bill, which is cosponsored by twenty-one other senators, John Tunney of California said, "There is substantial evidence that part-time workers are more efficient and productive than those in comparable full-time jobs . . . they often show more enthusiasm for the job and are less distracted by outside responsibilities. . . ."

That should encourage you if you have felt that people do not appreciate part-time workers. Among the volunteer opportunities, how about your own church? Or, for related service, there is: People caring. People sharing. People giving. People growing. This defines a home-missions emphasis known as PROP (Program for Retired Optional Personnel). PROP calls for a two-year commitment for service in home missions.

Farther afield, there is VISTA—with its opportunities for aiding the underprivileged in depressed areas in our own country, both city and rural.

Still farther, the Peace Corps beckons. A man came to hang draperies for us a few years ago. His speech betrayed his foreign background, and as we chatted, he confided that he would not be hanging drapes for the rest of his life. "This country has treated me so well [he was a refugee from Europe] that now I've applied to work with the Peace Corps overseas. I'm just waiting to be called." He must have been at least sixty.

Did you know that there is a Christian "Peace Corps"? Its name is INTERCRISTO (Box 9323, Seattle, Washington 98109. Toll-free number for personnel: 800-426-0506). Its purpose is to match needs of Christian organizations—both in America and around the world —with volunteer skills. INTERCRISTO maintains a file of those who have indicated their willingness to engage in certain work for specified lengths of time. They offer a free filing service for nonprofit Christian organizations. Until the emergence of this forward-looking organization, the means of meeting existing needs have been hit or miss. Now, through INTERCRISTO, we can be as wise as the "children of this world," as Jesus bade us be (*see* Luke 16:8). But it only works as those who have needs and desires let them be known.

There are fascinating jobs on the mission field. I personally know an orthopedic surgeon and his wife who recycled from California to Bangladesh. Now, almost through with their first year's language study, Dr. and Mrs. John Bullock have already been responsible for making available to these people not only what medicine and surgery can do, but also a limb-and-brace shop. In a country where crippled, handicapped people have no access to much that we have in this country, such an undertaking will bless thousands, making them productive persons rather than dependent *non*persons. And with it is spread the Gospel of Jesus Christ—who showed special concern for the lame.

We spoke earlier of activating a dream. In Bangkok this year, I met a lovely "retired" woman who isn't really retired. Most of her life she had dreamed of being a missionary, but home responsibilities and an ailing mother had prevented her. Then, free and healthy and willing, she had recycled her secretarial skills to Asia. She is happy, personally fulfilled, and contributing greatly. From personal observation, I would say that this kind of work has been grossly overlooked in planning mission personnel. For there is no less need of efficient secretaries in a hospital, literature department, bookstore, church, or school on the mission field than there is here in the homeland. I have seen nurses, doctors, lab technicians, evangelists, and others bogged down with work that a trained secretary could whip through in a few hours.

I know the former mayor of a California city who, long before his retirement, had planned to recycle his accountancy training to his denominational college for one year, then to Bangladesh. He and his wife spent long hours studying how best they could serve the Lord in their retirement years.

My own intent, if God so leads, is to present myself—with whatever I have to offer—to train nationals to write for their own people. Already this year I have done a stint in Hong Kong, Laos, Thailand, and Bangladesh. The people themselves can best write to the hearts of their own countrymen. With training they can be more successful in this than the finest missionary can hope to be. It is an exciting prospect to me!

This book came into being partly because one man cared enough for a college buddy to urge him to recycle his language-teaching skill, to travel abroad and give help to missionaries in their translating of the Scriptures. This is a crucial area of need for some missionaries who never expected to find themselves, of necessity, translators. The difficulty arises if they have not had adequate training in the original languages. Here, such a language professor can make an eternal contribution in his retirement years.

Probably one of the most strategic needs in our food-crisis world is for the trained agricultural missionary. An experienced farmer can, by spending a year or so, do much to launch a program and train nationals in productive methods. One mission board specializing in cooperative work with evangelical missionaries is FARMS, Inc. (123 West 57th, New York, N.Y. 10019).

I came across an ad in a magazine some weeks ago. It intrigued me.

HELP WANTED

1 person to advise an ox-plowing program
   in Sudan
1 sawmill supervisor for Nepal
1 horticulturalist for Botswana

1 principal for Beit Jala School on the
West Bank of Jordan
1 mine air researcher for Appalachia

These are some of unusual personnel needs on the list of service opportunities issued by the Mennonite Central Committee. They go on to list "more conventional skills" needed: medical, clerical, social, engineering, and all kinds of teaching. People are urged to send for a complete list—"It might help you to find out what the Lord has in store for you in the next few years."

ACTION (Agency for Volunteer Service, Washington, D.C. 20525), a Washington-based organization with regional offices in ten states, offers a variety of opportunities.

The Foster Grandparent Program is open to men or women sixty years old, in good health, and with low income. One "grandfather" writes, "I spent a lot of lonesome hours before I joined the program, but now I have something to look forward to. . . ."

Each grandparent is assigned two children and devotes two hours a day to each child. An hourly stipend is paid, and other benefits are part of the program. Some of the children are in institutions and hospitals.

Another facet of ACTION is its Senior Companion Program. This entails caring for shut-ins or for elderly persons in nursing homes. It is a two-way street, for as some of these senior companions have found, sharing of one's self with others brings both satisfaction and a cure for "separation" from the world.

A third group is ACTION's Retired Senior Volunteer Program (RSVP). Here are opportunities to assist teachers in classrooms (teaching what the person knows from a lifetime of experience, possibly "shop" or sewing, cooking, and so on). RSVP also works in hospitals, libraries, and facilities for mentally or physically handicapped children. To quote the pamphlet, "At RSVP, we think you've got a lot to give. If you think so too, get on the phone today."

We mentioned a number of organizations. These and others like them are useful and have value for certain people. However, don't think you need an organization to help you recycle into a worthwhile future. There is something special about praying for direct guidance, and then following as God opens a door.

I am reminded of a couple, the husband an all-round handyman, the wife a schoolteacher. In their fifties, they loaded their car (having sold their little home) and started out for an area in the Southwest where there were needs they could meet. There is a black community where the pastor and his wife are making a fine impact, and this white couple just fitted right in. Fred builds and fixes things, gardens, and is generally "available," his genial personality and wry humor adding to the enjoyment of those alongside as he works. He is creative; if he lacks the right tool, that's no problem—he just makes what he needs from whatever materials are on hand. Meanwhile Margaret loves and tutors numerous children. She arranges music lessons for them (and finds used pianos to be delivered to the homes of ambitious youngsters who will practice). In short, she looks for needs and finds ways to meet them. Between the two, no organization could ever afford this couple's services. They literally and figuratively beautify every place they touch.

When they arrived in this depressed area, the man in charge of the post office predicted aloud to them, "You won't last three months." Recently Fred wrote, "Last time I was in the post office he wasn't there; *he* is gone."

Perhaps this post-office worker was just being realistic. Lots of people cannot stand to be transplanted to where the soil is less favorable or even downright inhospitable. But—and I have proven this for myself—*when God calls and offers an opportunity for service,* the conditions somehow do not matter. (Our city friends used to openly pity us in our first pastorate in northern Ontario, while we who had been called there, reveled in it, even with physical inconveniences and bone-chilling cold.)

God has lots of job opportunities. He is just waiting for the applicants who will say, like Isaiah, ". . . . Here am I; send me" (Isaiah 6:8). No one ever regrets taking up God's offers.

A current advertisement for VISTA has as its punch line: "I gave a piece of my mind to [and a needy place is named]"—then a number of opportunities are presented.

Isn't this what opportunities are all about? We can give a piece of our *mind.* We can give a piece of our *heart.* We can give a piece of our *time.* We can give of our *finances.* We can give of *ourselves.*

To the person who would ask, "Why should I?" an answer has been given by Mrs. Dorothy Haskin of Friendship Mission: "If not I, who? If not now, when?"

Happiness is—reaching out to other people. The Apostle Paul reminded us that Jesus said so: "It is more blessed to give than to receive" (*see* Acts 20:35). How profound in its ramifications!

Attitude is the key to reaching out. We will never seek, recognize, and grasp recycling opportunities until we have the positive attitude that life has more for us—*that the future is ours.*

11

When You Can't Get Up

He has the right to criticize who has the heart to help.

Abraham Lincoln

At a social function a number of church people were discussing the recent loss of two of their members. Both men had died of lingering cancer. The conversation, very naturally, veered to the two new widows. At one point a woman remarked, "I just can't understand it. There's Sarah. She's taken her husband's death so well. But Joan!"— she rolled her eyes—"You'd think she isn't even a *Christian.*"

"I know," one of the men agreed. "I've wondered about that, too. And it bothers me. Maybe we haven't been as supportive of Joan as we have been of Sarah. Perhaps—"

"Nothing of the kind," a third person chipped in. "We've done everything we possibly could for each of them. I just feel that Sarah is showing her faith by rising above her grief, and Joan is wallowing in hers."

A few others joined in the discussion. For the most part they were compassionate toward the two women and voiced their desire to help as much as they could. But running through the talk was a thread of wondering why two people in the same straits were reacting so differently.

Some time ago, while I was interviewing a psychologist, Dr. Gary Collins, this topic surfaced. I had asked, "Can you explain why some Christians have a need for professional counseling and others do not? I mean, take two Christians seemingly at the same level of spiritual maturity. Both suffer an extreme loss. One bounces back emotionally and the other goes under. What are the dynamics at work in each case?"

Dr. Collins's reply was:

Actually there can be a number of factors. Certainly our background experiences are an important part. One may have had just so much stress that this is the last straw. She can't handle one more thing. The other, who has also had much stress, has built up a tolerance so that she is able to cope more than the other.

The personality also has a great bearing on our reactions. Because of temperament and undoubtedly because of learning through experience, one person can stay afloat when another would tend to sink. This is no reflection on the latter's spirituality.

Also, because of our interests and our background we respond differently. Here, for instance, are two men whose wives die. One man turns to God in his time of grief and the other rebels against God for taking away his helpmeet. Are we to say that one is more spiritual than the other because they respond differently? Many circumstances may enter in, and we must be careful not to judge people on the assumption that he who stands stress the longest is the most spiritual. It may be that he is not facing up to the problem the way the other man is; the person who "takes it so well" may indeed be in need of counseling more than the other who is facing up to the fact that he does have a problem.

The same might well be true of the two widows whose behavior was such an enigma to their church associates; one "taking it so well," the other virtually crying (if people had ears to hear), "Help me! I can't get up."

I have long realized that we sift each new happening in our lives through all the earlier experiences we have known. It figures, then, that faced with the same circumstance, two women's reactions can differ; one may show intense emotion, for instance, while the other maintains a stoic calm.

We should get it clear in our minds that there is nothing wrong with displaying emotions. God gave us our emotions. Sometimes the Christian church appears to frown on such expression, but this would have to be contrary to the nature of God, as revealed in both the Old and the New Testament. Jesus displayed emotion. Jesus wept—He did not repress His tears at the grave of His friend Lazarus. Yet how often His followers today express admiration for the person who "doesn't cry" or who "bears up" when sorrow comes.

While the film *The Hiding Place* was showing in my area I heard many people's responses to it. "I cried when I saw it," quite a few admitted. "I *didn't,*" one person differed. "I almost did, but I was able to control myself and keep from crying."

Is it an achievement to "keep from crying" when it would be quite appropriate to do so? Is there something "wrong" about weeping when something moves us?

A man of my acquaintance said to his wife, "You know I'll cry if I go to [a certain place], and you wouldn't like that."

I should say that this man is no weakling—far from it! And how do you think his wife responded? "Don't you know that this is one of the things I love you for—that you *can* cry."

If, then, one woman cries and another "bears up" when her husband dies, we need to be understanding of both. Far be it from one Christian to criticize another for his or her emotional responses. Rather, we can offer help. Sometimes the very best thing one person does for another at such times—when the bereaved feels she just cannot rise above the grief—is to kindly suggest that professional help would be advisable.

Frequently, it does not help one bit to seek out a minister (which a high percentage of people do at such times). Reluctant as some of them might be to admit it, many pastors are not equipped by training to deal with any but surface emotional problems. Oh, there are some who have been God-endowed with a rare, intuitive sensitivity. But even they will admit that if the problem is severe, it calls for professional help. Other ministers, in addition to not being trained counselors, cannot handle emotional problems for this reason: they are predisposed to resist anything that can't be "cured" or that will not go away with only an application of the reading from the Bible and/or "a word of prayer." They may be the finest of pastors in every other respect.

As a minister's wife for some thirty years, I know what I'm talking about. No minister of the Gospel was ever more loving and compassionate toward his congregation than Rev. E. A. Lockerbie, as a host of people would testify. The door of our home was open, as well as the church study, and people came to both with their problems at all hours. Not always were they deep concerns, and I assume that most left with a lighter heart than when they came.

Sometimes—*when it was appropriate*—I was called in before the interview concluded, and quite often my husband would suggest I read a few verses of Scripture. Then either he or I would pray. At times—and I couldn't have explained it to myself then—I had a nagging sense that this was not enough, that unless something had been said during the interview that would lift the burden, the person would carry out the same load he or she had carried in. Not only so, but there could be an added weight, for as Christians we believe (and rightly so) that the Word of God and praying to God is our special resource. Therefore, when it doesn't seem to "work," our thinking is: *It must be me.* We feel that God has hidden His face from us, and our desolation is all the greater.

People who work with Christians who have emotional problems tell me that such feelings are common. The depressed person admits to feeling guilty because he does not find the answer to his problems in the Bible or as he prays. Some even fearfully confess their anger against God. My Christian-psychologist friends tell me that such people can see only the Bible verses that "beat them over the head" —verses about the wrath and judgment of God, rather than those that speak of His love and compassion, His healing concern. (I suspect that it was out of such experiences, and to help these people, that Dr. Bruce Narramore and Bill Counts wrote the book *Guilt and Freedom.*)

What is the commonsense recourse for people suffering from emotional problems which keep them from being able to face life? Obviously the answer is a specialist trained in this area. To look to a minister of the Gospel to supply the remedy for something that does not have a spiritual cause is putting too much of a burden on him— and you are not doing yourself a service. Would you take your aching tooth to an allergist? Or your fractured arm to a dermatologist?

We can thank God that in our day He has raised up a whole new area of help: men and women who believe in Christ, seek to live by His Word, and whose training in psychology qualifies them to counsel. Nobody needs to go through life "unable to get up." The first thing is to recognize the need for such help. Then—*don't be talked out of it.*

I notice two differing attitudes toward psychologists or psychiatrists. On the one hand it seems to be a fad, the "in" thing. Some people speak of "my therapist" as they do their dentist or their travel agent—very openly, as though everybody has one. There are others who would prefer to hide the fact that they are seeing a counselor. To them there appears to be something unacceptable to society, something of a stigma about seeking help for emotional problems. As we have indicated, this is particularly true in the Christian community, for it seems to deny the power of God. Of course it does not!

A thousand times worse is the attitude that, in sending trials, God is punishing the person. Therefore he should be willing to endure it as a kind of penance, rather than seeking help. There are people who feel it is a disgrace to have trouble descend on them. Obviously they will not be in the market for help for this would mean exposing the problem. So they rob themselves and probably affect those who are close to them, for what we are rubs off on other people.

The question is sometimes asked: "What does a professional counselor have to offer that a trusted friend couldn't give just as well?" And it is a good question.

One thing is *objectivity.* A professional listens without taking sides when another person is involved. He listens without judging or condemning or just giving advice. He does not deal in *shoulds*—what one should or should not do. Through his training and experience he helps the person get at the root cause of his problem. Then, as a medical doctor can prescribe only after he has diagnosed the case, the psychologist can move into helpful therapy, enabling the client to "get up and go on," rather than being a dropout from life.

In earlier days, people had time for one another. Life was not so harried, so pressured. This is something I also discussed with Dr. Collins. "Before the era of modern psychology," I asked him, "how did we get along. What was the "psychology" that helped keep people on an even keel emotionally? Or is it that our generation is in worse shape than any other that preceded it, and God has brought psychological help into being for such a time?"

Dr. Collins's reply to my question was:

> Psychology is a science, and I don't know why the Lord didn't bring it to the fore earlier. But let me say that for centuries there has been an emphasis on pastoral counseling, and on listening and sharing one another's problems.
>
> Then, too, we need to consider that we are living in a knowledge-explosion era. This increased scientific and technological know-how tends to produce great stress. We are a success-oriented people, and this success motivation colors our behavior; we have a generation of rushing-around people. We're busy—busy —busy, until this has become a way of life. (Perhaps this *busy-ness* is to compensate for a somewhat empty life in spite of all we appear to have going for us as Americans.)
>
> It would appear we have more need than did earlier generations for the skills of the psychologist and psychiatrist, and God in His wisdom has raised up this avenue of human help just when it was most needed.

I agree thoroughly that there has historically been ongoing "counseling." It used to be called by a less high-sounding term: *neighboring.* Many a problem has been lessened as people have talked and others have listened to them. Almost every community had—and some still have—those individuals who are natural counselors. They have a genuine concern for other people, and because of their empathetic nature they attract to themselves other people's problems. They may never have read one page of a psychology book or taken any course in counseling. Nevertheless, they have an almost uncanny sense of what to say—and not say—what to do to really help the person who needs their help in a time of emotional stress.

There is a snare to watch out for, however. Not everyone who is available as a listener should be considered as a source of help. Some disturbed people have found to their hurt that the listener who is so understanding and has so much time to offer is really meeting his or her own need to be needed. The sympathetic ear may thrive on other people's problems and obtain gratification from being a repository of the spilled-over emotions of a friend or neighbor. So, before taking advantage of the openhanded help of such a counselor, it will be wise to pause and ask yourself, "Is he wanting to meet my needs—or his own?"

Usually this kind of counselor is at least as needy as the one being supposedly helped. Moreover, since such an advisor actually needs the person *not* to get over the problem, he or she will tend to cause the "client" to see the problem as somebody else's fault, to fix blame apart from the client. This can never help. Only facing up to the real causes can be a step toward release and relief. Another factor to consider is this: If the person you confide in has a neurotic need to be needed, is it not likely that such a person will have to tell other people in order to obtain gratification? And confidentiality is inherent and necessary in real counseling.

So—watch it, when you feel you must spill out some of the feelings that are poisoning you! You can never recall your words. However, don't let the fact that some listeners are not competent to counsel keep you from appropriating the help of one who can and will help you resolve your problems.

When we can feel free to open up and talk about the things that are on our mind, we begin to work through and spell out what we are thinking and *feeling*. Often, as we do, we are sifting our thoughts and clarifying them for ourselves. Sometimes we have really not mulled over the ramifications of a problem because we have not had someone to whom we could talk about it—really talk, without having the feeling that "I'm taking too much of your time," or "You wouldn't be interested in hearing about this."

If we could get back to having time for one another, instead of being ships passing in the night, we might not need the professionals except for severe problems.

This was underscored for me a few weeks ago. On a Saturday afternoon, an old friend (I'll call her Sue) phoned me. She was clearly very upset. Before she had even begun to explain what was troubling her, I said, "Sue, do you feel like coming to my house? We could sit down and talk over whatever it is that's upsetting you." She grasped at my invitation as though she were desperate, and she is usually a calm, very levelheaded woman. When she arrived we went out to a quiet restaurant for dinner so that we could sit undisturbed, and she poured out her story. It was long and with a number of ramifications. I listened, only very occasionally saying something. We went back to my home and sat in the living room for an hour or two, still discussing the problem. As we did, it began to come untangled. My friend became more relaxed; she even smiled.

Why am I telling you all this? Because of what she said as we parted later that evening. With a sudden liveliness—just like her real self, and as though a great truth had just struck her—Sue exclaimed, "Everything's exactly the same as it was when I came. Nothing about the circumstances has changed. *But everything is different.* It's going to be all right. I feel I can handle it."

Sometimes this is all it takes. We can help each other up. There are problems, however, that are too severe for people. They cannot rise above them. No use saying to them, "Try to forget, and go on," or any other kindly intended exhortation. Most people would get up if they could, following a knockdown blow. When things are too much for them on their own—well, we can thank God that He has provided counselors.

There are times when the most long-range help we can be to an emotionally troubled friend is to support him or her as one seeks the right kind of professional help. I believe God is *for* Christian counseling. After all, one of the names given to Jesus is Counselor.

The right kind of counseling can be the route to recovery and to worthwhile recycling of all the person's God-given potential.

12

Recycling With a Goal

A goal is a dream spelled out.

In our younger years other people establish our goals. Sometimes it is not until we are fifty plus that we find we can activate a dream and turn it into a goal. I would like to suggest that you pause—stop right now—and thoughtfully ask yourself, "What have I always dreamed of doing?"

Then, if for reasons of retirement, health, change of location, or any other factor, recycling is in order for you, ask yourself another question: "What is keeping me from moving in the direction of what I would most like to do?" You may then want to consider some of the things we have discussed so far: polishing up your skills, taking new training, availing yourself of social or vocational opportunities, and so on.

Until we have a goal, life can be just a going around in circles. Makes me think of a scene in *Alice in Wonderland.* Alice had met up with the Cheshire cat and asked him for directions. As I recall, the conversation went something like this:

ALICE: Please tell me which way I should go from here.
CAT: Depends on where you want to go.
ALICE: I really don't care where I go.
CAT: Then it doesn't matter which way you go.

Nothing can so contribute to a sense of futility as not having a place to go, for how do we know when we are halfway there or, for that matter, when we arrive? We don't know which landmarks to take for direction or which pitfalls to avoid.

"It's the realistic goals you set for your life that can give it meaning and fulfillment," says psychiatrist Dr. Roy W. Menninger. I like Dr. Menninger's modifying "realistic." Goals we cannot reasonably attain are probably worse than none. Why? Because even in the setting of goals for ourselves there is a certain excitement and anticipation. Then, when we find we cannot make it (for whatever reason) our spirits droop lower than they were before we had any goal in view.

One of the problems, therefore, about goal setting stems from the individual's aiming for something unrealistic. I see this occasionally in a woman with an emphasis on housecleaning. She decides to do the whole house. So she hauls things out of closets and drawers and cupboards and goes at it to meet her goal. But even before noon she is so tired that the project goes slower and slower. By mid-afternoon she is exhausted and surrounded by all the clutter and doesn't know which way to turn. "I should never have started this in the first place," she groans. But *starting* it was not the problem. Having an unrealistic goal was what did her in. I know, for I've tried this and I know where it got me. The true satisfaction, I find, is in deciding to do a piece of the work and finish it. The same is true of the amateur gardener who plows into the job and, because he goes at it too hard the first day, can barely move the next day. So he gives up.

Some people set about to activate a dream of becoming an artist. They indulge in a spending spree for oils and brushes and canvases. But they may not be realistic about starting at the bottom, so they become easily discouraged. Not only have they not attained their dream but they have lost money in the process. There are, however, many who do set realistic goals, and their lives are enriched as they move toward fulfillment and realization of their dreams.

Achievement usually costs perseverance over the things that would discourage and daunt us. Therefore I like the words Booker T. Washington left us: "Success is to be measured not so much by the position that one has reached in life as by the obstacles which he has overcome while trying to succeed."

It should be said that *we don't always succeed.* Having a goal does not ensure the achieving of it. But how much better to set a goal and strive for it than, as is facetiously said, "to aim at nothing and succeed."

I remember blinking a time or two at what I was reading in the classified ads in a Bengali newspaper. It was in the JOBS WANTED category. More than one would-be employee described his qualifications for a position as "B.A. (Failed)." I had heard people joking about this, but I didn't know it was true. Actually there is nothing about it that should make us laugh. Here is a person, usually a young man, who has somehow managed to get through high school and to be accepted in a college. He had even taken exams, but these he had failed. This did not, however, take away from him the years of study. He was advertising himself as being head and shoulders above his fellow job seekers who had never attended college or university. Failing the exams was just a part of his experience and not the most important part. (It could be that such a person didn't have access to the right textbooks because of a shortage in that country, or he may have had no way of getting to the place where the exams were given —and thus he "failed.")

Another thing about goals is to keep in mind that they should not be permitted to control us totally—that is, goals for their own sake. It is not the goal that is so all-important. There must be satisfaction along the way toward this goal. There are people who seemingly go through life only for a goal they have set off in the future. It is never today, but some far-off tomorrow when they expect to enjoy life— "When the house is paid for"—"When the kids are grown"—"When I retire"—"When I have enough money." My minister-brother says, *"Enough* money is always more than the person has." This would say to me that the one who makes money his goal in life will never arrive. He will never have enough. Even so, he will mortgage today's enjoyment to pay for that mirage of tomorrow.

As in every area of life, making goals has to have a balance. And we are all the more likely to stick with our goal over the long haul if we segment it into short-term aims which we can enjoy in the meantime. For example, I am frequently asked, "How do you ever get a book written?" Generally the question has little or nothing to do with technique and procedure. Rather, the person (often a writer or would-be writer) may be voicing a longing: "I wish I could stick with it and finish a book [or some other project] I start."

I am glad to share with such people that I, too, would likely have difficulty if I thought of a writing project as "doing a book." I start out knowing what the book will be about—where it is going—and then I chop it into chapter topics. This is like getting through today, rather than assuming the burdens of a whole lifetime. God favors this kind of thinking. He promises us: ". . . as thy days, so shall thy strength be" (Deuteronomy 33:25).

It was with this comforting thought in mind that I wrote these lines from "The Gift of Today and Tomorrow."

> But our God, He who made us
> Knows just what we need,
> That "Time" is too long
> Without segments
> And courage breaks—and so on;
> So in love and in wisdom
> He gave us the gift
> Of time as "today" and "tomorrow."

Probably, if we could borrow tomorrow's strength in a kind of credit-card fashion—"Use today and pay tomorrow"—we would do just that. But in His wisdom God apportions us *by the day* what we need for the day.

Because I see the chapters as pieces that I can handle, these short-term goals can be achieved. First thing I know I have reached my long-term goal: the book is completed!

Again let me say that we do not always follow through to the completion of our goal. Sometimes this is dependent on other people or on circumstances beyond our own control which we could not foresee when we established the goal. I was caused to think of this one day this week when I heard someone say, "I've done everything I can on this project, but the people doing the next part just aren't cooperating." To my surprise, the other person, an efficient supervisor, suggested, "Check it off as incomplete." I grinned a bit over that; then the thought struck me that it was probably a good suggestion. When we have done all we can, then we have a right to check it off, not to feel that we have failed.

For the good feeling that success gives us, we all need to have short-term as well as long-term goals. Obvious achievement also tends to motivate other people. It seems to me that I have lived most of my life with goal-oriented people. As a minister's wife I recall with deep satisfaction the things we planned and, with the help of the Lord, saw through to completion. An instance stands out in my mind. We had just finished a tremendous missionary conference. The missionary speakers had outdone themselves; the people had responded with great dedication; the financial goal was exceeded. A high spirit of jubilation made eyes shine. It was as though everybody present had established goals and each one of them had been reached. The crowd had thinned until just a few of the church officials were standing around enthusing, when one of them said, "Okay, pastor, what do you have cooking for us next?" They reveled in the success they had been a part of, and they were ready to go to the next undertaking. It is always easier to motivate helpers when they can see we have a defined goal, that we know where we are heading and have a plan for getting there.

Working with the Apostle Paul must have been like this. He knew where he was going. He speaks of "one thing I do" (not a buckshot approach) and "I press toward the mark for the prize" (*see* Philippians 3:13, 14). It was not the reward itself that kept Paul pressing on. It was what was involved in winning the prize—it was a contest which *Jesus* had initiated. He is the One who will judge and award the prizes for faithful proclaiming of the Gospel. We can all get in on it, for there is no closing date for entering—until Jesus comes. How exciting to realize that we will be there (if we have trusted Jesus as our Saviour), and I imagine that in addition to rewards there will be some surprizes. Some who have never made earth's headlines just may find themselves away up front.

Maybe we need to think about goals in our *service for Christ.* It is commendable to have a concern for the whole world for which Jesus died. But—let's face it—most of us cannot "go into all the world and preach the gospel to every creature" (*see* Mark 16:15). We would have to be on worldwide television with everybody tuned in, to accomplish that. But there are our neighbors and the milkman and the newsboy and the mailman. (Oh, don't neglect your *mailman;* he brings you good news lots of times!)

If it is success we are looking for—And who isn't?—recycling some of our time into working for God brings guaranteed results. I was recently impressed as a woman who has been a Christian just a very short time said with great conviction, *"I believe God;* I believe His promises, and He has promised to be with me and help me when I go out to tell my friends and neighbors about Christ and what He's doing for me every day." She is walking enthusiasm for God. She dashes into my office on her coffee break and asks, "Jeanette, did you get something today that will help me in my spiritual life?" (One of her duties is to deliver the mail around the offices, so she knows I get gobs of this and that.) Sometimes she pops in and asks, "Have you a minute?" and shares some new blessing—or a problem she is having in witnessing. We talk it over, and then she gives me a quick hug and she is on her way back to her desk. *Such people must bring joy to the heart of Jesus,* I often think.

Since goal setting and following through obviously pay dividends in personal fulfillment, why would a person not be interested?

"I'm too tired!" is often the reason given. Doubtless most of us are in that category. We all get tired at times. But not tired *all* the time.

There are two kinds of "tired"—the healthy kind we feel when, after doing some physical task that called for more than usual effort, we stretch and say, "Well, *that's* done!" It's a good feeling even though a muscle or two may be protesting. This is a tiredness which normal rest will cure.

The other kind of "tired" is much more of a problem. Let me say that this tiredness may have a physical cause and the person would be well-advised not to just tolerate it, but to see a physician. We should be careful about lumping all tired people together and criticizing them, indicting them for using their fatigue as an excuse to evade responsibility. Usually we cannot know what causes another person to do what he does or doesn't do.

There is a healthy "tired" and a "tired" that cannot be explained in terms of health, the latter a chronic weariness. As we have seen, the healthy tiredness stems from meaningful activity. The chronic type? Although it incapacitates people, experts cannot pinpoint its cause. Sometimes it can be observed in people who, in addition to being tired—tired—tired, are busy—busy—busy. This is a driving kind of "busy" that yet never quite gets a thing accomplished. Therefore the person never attains the gratification of sitting down and viewing a job well done.

Women as well as men suffer from this kind of tiredness. The men bring work home from the office. They almost never relax, yet their work never gets done and they complain of being tired all the time. The women have a stack of ironing or other household chores constantly undone. Yet they work at it, never having the satisfaction of knowing they can relax with the knowledge that their work is in good shape. These are people who can say, "I haven't a lazy bone in my body." Maybe they are trying to prove it. Who knows?

Another theory as to the cause of chronic tiredness is that the person is bored, just plain bored with living. It has been said that boredom is more subtle than sin; the conscience doesn't warn against it. Boredom is a disease that erodes initiative and shrivels personality. It robs the individual of the joy the Lord meant us to have and withers our capacity for serving Him. And while almost every major disease these days has a campaign going to help eradicate it, not so with the disease of boredom. Yet it is a killjoy that handicaps millions.

I am not thinking of the boredom many of us have known—a *temporary* feeling of monotony toward a job, person, conversation. Almost anything can bore us at times. It is the *permanent* lack of interest in anything that is the joy killer we need to guard ourselves against and help other people do likewise.

Authorities cite various reasons such as *selfishness* and *lack of motivation*. But whether these and other reasons we might speculate on are cause or effect, no one seems to know, because this disease of boredom is in the realm of those mysterious elements: personality and the subconscious.

Oddly, conditions that bore one person can stimulate another. Consider the case of two women I know (names are changed): Sarah Adams and Hannah Lane were both widowed in their late fifties. Sarah made no effort to adjust to her new circumstances. She stayed home, complained of being tired all the time, and seemingly wallowed in self-pity. Her subsequent boredom led to a persecution complex. She became demanding and made life miserable for everybody who tried to help her. She refused to be interested in or to enjoy anything

—until she began to be thought of as a nuisance by some.

Contrast her response to her changed circumstance with Hannah's attitude in the same situation. Hannah was, in some people's opinion, also a bit of a nuisance. For Hannah was "nosy," they said. They were right. She was nosy enough to find out about an elderly couple, both blind and in need of someone to do a number of things for them that they could not do for themselves. Hannah became eyes for them. She became their link with the seeing world as she helped with correspondence with their loved ones, among many other thoughtful things she did for the couple. And that was just the beginning of what kept this widow from being bored.

Though the experts cannot agree as to what causes boredom, they do agree on the conditions that nurture it: *leisure time* and *nothing to do*. Perhaps in this recognition lies both the prevention and cure: keeping busy in mind and body. It is significant that generally it is the mind that gives up before the body. I've talked this over with an athletic coach who agreed, "Of course. It's the mind that signals the body to quit." No doubt this explains the term "psyching ourselves into [or out of] something"—as an athlete "psyching" himself into winning a race, his mind telling his body to keep on and win, although the body feels "I can't."

Selfishness and a lack of motivation—if these are the culprits in producing boredom, then the solution ought to be simple: *unselfishness* and *motivation*. This brings us back to the matter of goals. All anyone has to do is to look around for opportunities to demonstrate unselfishness in both big and little ways every day. I know, for example, a woman who lives in a rather poor neighborhood. She has a front yard with no fence and a lot of flowers she tends herself. A friend visiting her remarked about the lovely flowers and added, "But they're so near the sidewalk. Don't the neighborhood children pick them?"

"That's why I planted them there," the woman answered. "These children have so little that is pretty. I want them to enjoy the flowers, so I'm happy when they pick them."

In this simple way one woman displayed both unselfishness and motivation. She also had a goal the day she planted the seeds. This formula: UNSELFISHNESS + MOTIVATION + GOAL will almost invariably conquer boredom.

Not always must the goal be in the interests of other people, however. We also need goals that have our own interests at their core. Remember that Jesus said we should love other people *as we love ourselves,* so we need to show love to ourselves. In this connection, I have a very good friend from whom I keep learning some great lessons. Ruth works with Jewish people, for whom she has truly unconditional love. One of these women, named Gladys, has had tremendous problems all her life, and after months of loving attention and a lot of prayer, she learned to trust Jesus as her Saviour. She still had a way to go emotionally—and she needed a lot of buildup. Ruth is an expert in this department and when she leaves after spending some time with this woman, Ruth will say to her, "And remember, take care of Gladys!" That was a new thought to me and it has true merit. We need to do the things (and *not* do some other things) with a view to how they can contribute to our own well-being.

Personally I find that having something to look forward to chases any feelings of temporary boredom. Happy anticipation can sometimes be as satisfying as the treat itself. We do need to give ourselves pleasures to anticipate. So that should be one of our goals. If it sounds selfish to you, think again of how, by "loving" yourself, you are likely to be developing attitudes that will help you to be more loving to your neighbor.

These treats can be quite simple, but they must have meaning for *you.* For instance, a friend of mine who has a weight problem and has to constantly watch her diet, nevertheless permits herself an occasional piece of her favorite brand of chocolates. "I can stand all this," she says (indicating the lettuce and carrots and such), "because I have *this,* " and she brings out her special candy. For me the big temptation is not to overeat, but to over *read.* My eyes are not the best, and I need them in my profession, apart from general use. So I promise myself that when I have accomplished a certain goal, I can—*without any guilt feelings*—sit down with a good book for an hour or two. The anticipation helps me to discipline myself to keep on target.

The treat can, of course, be something major such as a trip abroad. This kind offers weeks, perhaps months, of travel-folder enjoyment, an armchair tour before you set out. Whatever the thing anticipated, it is true in my own and other people's experiences that "things go better" when one can look forward to a special delight.

Any goal should include planned rest—the relaxation of change. Jesus exemplified the need for this when He established the very first Christian Retreat. His disciples were emotionally torn up due to the death of John the Baptist. Crowds pressed on them hour after hour, and meeting human needs robbed them of time even to eat. Some had been out preaching and teaching and doubtless were weary.

> Then Jesus suggested, "Let's get away from the crowds for a while and rest." . . . So they left by boat for a quieter spot.
>
> Mark 6:31, 32 LB

It did not prove to be much of a rest, for the crowds had a way of finding the compassionate, miracle-working Jesus. Nevertheless, Christ forever put His seal on the value of rest following labor. There are Christians who emphasize that Christ told us to *work*. They stress the fact that He Himself worked tirelessly. And He did. But, as in everything else, Christ was perfectly balanced. He would not have us be "workaholics," and to offset this He provided a pattern for rest.

In summary—it is not God's will that we should *go aimlessly* through the rest of our lives. Neither is it His will that we should *be tired* day after day. It is certainly not His will that we should so demean the creativity He has given us as to *be bored* with life from now on.

Having some well-defined goal—activating a dream—can be the antidote to disenchantment with life when you are fifty plus.

Now what *was* that thing you decided you most wanted to do as you recycle? *You can achieve anything which God plants in your heart and mind as a goal.*

13

The Best Days of Your Life

I grow old learning something new every day.

Solon

When is the best time in life?

Ask any child and he'll tell you, "It's when I grow up, so I can do all the things nobody will let me do now." My grandmother used to tell us children, when we talked in this vein, "You're just wishing your life away." That would tell me in retrospect that my grandmother figured the best time in her life had been during her earlier days. Yet the child looks ahead and dreams—*Wait till I'm big.* The future looms so full of promise of things denied him now. But he may look back later and declare that his childhood was the best time of his life.

Take the teenager. Surely this is the best time of life: free from the limiting frustrations of the younger child, not yet burdened with adult responsibilities, a whole exciting world beckoning. Nevertheless, many of us can recall the anxiety-laden teenage days. They were not the best days of our lives.

What of early adulthood with its sky-is-the-limit possibilities: love —marriage—a career? This *must* be the best time. But, no. This group as much as any other helps to flood the offices of psychiatrists and psychologists.

Then there is the life-begins-at-forty group. Perhaps it does for many people. Generally, though, the fortieth milestone makes little appreciable difference in the person or in his way of life.

Next we come to what I like to call the fruitful fifties. Again, some people find great contentment and enjoyment in these years; some do not. This latter group may be too busy living in the past to reap the benefits of the present.

It would appear that the best time in life for a great many people is always some other time than the present. *Yesterday* or *tomorrow* may hold more enchantment than their *today.* Surely God did not intend that this should be so.

Speaking to the fifty-plus segment, former Vice-President Hubert Humphrey said at age fifty-nine:

> This period can be one of the richest and most fulfilling. It is an age of re-evaluation and readjustment, where the idealistic and ambitious intensity of youth is replaced by a more realistic appraisal and deeper appreciation of life itself.

This positive attitude brings to mind an intriguing prayer I read some time ago. Titled "A Prayer for Older Folks," it has implications for any responsible person who is interested in enjoying good relationships with people. Age has very little to do with this quality of life.

> Lord, thou knowest that I am growing older.
> Keep me from becoming too talkative, and particularly keep me from falling into the tiresome habit of expressing an opinion on every subject.
> Release me from the craving to straighten out everybody's affairs.
> Keep my mind free from the recital of endless details. Give me wings to get to the point.
> Give me the grace, dear Lord, to listen to others describe their aches and pains. Help me to endure the boredom with patience and to keep my lips sealed. For my own aches and pains are increasing in number and intensity and the pleasure of discussing them is becoming sweeter as the years go by.
> Teach me the glorious lesson that, occasionally, I might be mistaken.
> Keep me reasonably sweet; I do not wish to be a saint (saints are so hard to live with) but a sour old woman is the crowning work of the devil.

Make me thoughtful, but not moody; helpful, but not pushy; independent, yet able to accept with graciousness favors that others wish to bestow upon me.

Free me of the notion that simply because I have lived a long time I am wiser than those who have not lived so long.

If I do not approve of some of the changes that have taken place in recent years, give me the wisdom to keep my mouth shut.

Lord, you know that when the end comes I would like to have a friend or two left. Amen!

INEZ SPENCE

This is my own daily prayer—every word of it. If it contains thoughts and aspirations that find an echo in your heart, too, then together we can begin to change in the ways we feel we need to. For parts of this interesting prayer *we can answer ourselves* (of course, using the resources God gives us for change). Our new attitudes will do so much to make every day of every year fruitful.

"No man is an island." What we are as men and women—our attitudes and behavior—affects very directly those who are close to us. To illustrate: Two children were visiting their grandparents which they did frequently, for the families lived just minutes from each other. But on this particular day the grandmother said, "Run outside and play, children. Don't bother your grandpa."

Rather disconsolately the brother and sister made their way out to the backyard. Their faces mirrored both disappointment and perplexity. When had they ever "bothered" Grandpa? He'd been the most fun!

"Wisht I knew what's wrong," Jack said. "Grandma didn't even give us a cookie, and Grandpa—"

"*I* know," Susie butted in, proud that she knew something her brother didn't. "It's *retirement;* that's what Grandpa has. I heard Mommy telling somebody, and she said it's making him grumpy."

"Wonder if he'll have it for a long time, or if it's like when we got the measles," the two speculated. Then they found consolation in a game with the neighbor kids.

Meanwhile the recently retired grandfather and his wife are living out one more day. Hanging between them, unsaid, are the questions:

"What's happening?"—"Wasn't this supposed to be the best time of our lives?"

Like many others, this fifty-plus couple has looked forward to this time of life. Free from the tyranny of the alarm clock five mornings a week, their time their own, they had expected retirement to be all that the ads portrayed it. When this highly touted Utopia-creating thing turns out to be less than satisfactory, disillusionment sets in. I suspect that if we would take a survey, we would find quite a high percentage of both men and women who do not view retirement as the best time of their lives. And sometimes this tends to sour their dispositions. If people around them are not sensitive to what is going on in the hearts and minds of the retired, it makes their behavior all the more difficult to understand.

How, for instance, could two children be expected to understand what was making their grandparents suddenly act differently toward them? Happily, the children's hope can be realized. The "retirement sickness" can be as temporary as a case of measles.

What might be some of the causes, the factors that uniquely affect a couple when the husband is retired? These are days when volumes are being written on the subject of communication. It would almost seem that if two people can *communicate,* they are assured a problem-free future, relationshipwise. There is more than a little truth in this, as many people will attest.

The couple whose attitudes so perplexed their grandchildren may never have had much going between them. Retirement will not automatically cut off communication; neither will it facilitate it. I might submit that, although they had so much time to spend together, they might as well have been on separate continents as far as being companionable and communicative is concerned.

Probably it was different when "John" had his job and "Mary" her interests. They had something to share when he came home from work. To be sure, the trend toward role reversal is with us, but it has not yet greatly affected today's fifty-plus couples.

The Roles of the Sexes

In many cases the wife is the one who will have to make a determined effort to see that retirement works for both of them. This should not be a hardship, for is it not one of the glories of being a woman? God made us to be helpmeets. There are things men need women to do for them and vice versa. It takes a woman to make a man feel he *is* a man in certain situations. Retirement affords great opportunities for a woman to demonstrate such understanding.

Quite often the wife's life-style has not changed too much with the years. She is still queen of her own realm. She is still needed; she has her responsibilities that are fulfilling to her. By contrast, her retired husband may feel he is in a vacuum which his job for so long has filled. He may be suffering from all kinds of feelings—from rejection to resentment to bitterness—even depression. Some women, meanwhile, are often concerned that they no longer have their domain all to themselves. I know more than one woman who has said, "All right. If he's going to hang around all day [As if it weren't his home, too!] he might as well do some of the work"—and she sets about to program his homework.

Some years ago in *Psychology for Living* I did a brief article titled "Letting the Retired Man Be a Man." Believe me, I got some flack from my readers. I appreciated their point of view, even though it was attacking my own on the subject. I'll share a part of the article here:

> Driving along one morning recently I noticed an elderly man, his arms encircling a bulging load, head into a laundromat. Naturally I had no way of knowing if the man was a person who lives alone and this was his own stuff. But, seeing him, my thoughts reverted back—back to another man; another scene.
>
> It was a day when my mother wasn't feeling well and Dad, after volunteering his help around the house added in his kindly way, "But just don't ask me to shake out the rugs—and I won't be hanging out the clothes" (it was before the days of "a vacuum and a clothes dryer" in every house in Scotland).
>
> My mother had undoubtedly heard little (more likely nothing) pertaining to psychology, but she understood intuitively what underlay her husband's spoken words: something like, *It's not that I mind helping out—but some things rob a man of his manliness.*

Traditionally, a man does man's work. He provides the living for his family; he "fixes things"; he shovels snow, washes the car, etc. With the contrariness of human nature, when Mother decides it's a good evening for eating dinner outdoors, Dad dons an apron and does the barbecueing—and it doesn't blur his manly image.

Whatever we might think of all of this, whatever Women's Lib may be doing to alter opinion, the fact remains that God made men to be men and women to be women.

How this concept is applied is generally a cultural thing. It would have been an unheard of thing among my father's people for a man to do "women's work"; shaking out rugs and hanging out clothes to dry fell into this category. And my mother wisely acknowledged it.

In the mature years the role of the sexes is just as important as it is at any other period of life. Yet, in how many instances do we find that the retired male appears to be expected to lay aside his masculinity! It is as though some women can hardly wait for the husband to retire so they can make a houseboy of him. Other women frankly admit that, after the initial pleasure of having their husband home most of the day, "I don't know what to do with him." The considerate wife will think twice, however, before getting her husband out from under her feet by sending him off to the laundromat to wrestle with detergents and water temperatures like the female star of a television commercial!

Before I get another flood of mail, let me be quick to explain that I am certainly not for the woman doing all the work and the husband sitting around with his newspaper. Far from it. Nor had I been subjected to such throughout my married life. I had the cooperation of my husband who was quick to recognize that I also had a part in his work in the church. He often openly expressed himself on this: "Why shouldn't I be willing to help with the dishes and such? My wife helps me." And when on occasion I used a laundromat, if he was home he would drive me there and carry in the laundry.

If I am crusading, it is not against cooperation. The Bible is clear that the husband is to *love* his wife. When he does, the cooperation is there. And certainly the retired husband and wife should do things together. But—and I am stating my own opinion in this—unless circumstances dictate otherwise, it is too much for a man when his wife delegates "woman's work" for him to do alone.

I think that children and even grandchildren can be affected by seeing a father or grandfather cast into a traditionally feminine role. He may be less looked up to by them; they may see him as a Casper Milquetoast character. This, in turn, can color their attitudes in their own homes.

Where *does* Dad fit in, in his retirement years?

Much will depend on his personality and his own concept of himself. Common sense would dictate that a man who has responsibly carried on at his business and profession should not at retirement relinquish his dignity in favor of becoming a combined household helper and errand boy. The man himself needs to guard positively against such a possibility. He can do this by providing for worthwhile pursuits—before he retires.

The husband and wife will do well to come to an understanding as to what each expects of the other. This is where communication is vital. The fact is that in allowing himself to become a chore boy, the retired man does neither himself nor his wife any favor. For, to be happy, a woman needs to be able to continue to look up to and respect her man. It is in *her* power, generally, to preserve her husband in his retirement years from becoming less of a man than he is.

There is so much they can do together. Some things are in her domain; some in his. Happy the couple when the woman recognizes the difference and refuses to stoop to using her husband as a kind of extension of herself. Not only will she then let him be a man, but she will encourage him in this. Both husband and wife are then likely to find a good measure of satisfaction and fulfillment.

Things Go Better With Planning

The wise Solomon wrote: "To every thing there is a season, and a time to every purpose under the heaven" (Ecclesiastes 3:1). We give mental assent to these insightful words, but to what practical use do we put this knowledge?

Recognition of the approaching "season of the fifty plus" and acknowledgment that God has a purpose for us in those years can make the difference between one's facing them calmly or being confronted by a crisis. It is good then for us to stop and consider, take stock of our present in the light of how it will affect our tomorrows. This will take in all areas of life, since we are integrated beings: physical, spiritual, and emotional. And we should not neglect the intellectual! A woman shared with me how she became impressed with the worth of maintaining a keen interest in learning. A trained nurse, one of her cases was a senile patient. Because she had worked with many such persons, she became curious as to the possible causes of this brand of mental problem. She did some research in a medical library and, to quote her: "I found one doctor who wrote in laymen's language. He said that if a person bound up his arm for years, you could imagine what would happen to it. In the same way, something happens to the parts of the brain which we do not use. Those cells actually die." This woman went on to say that her patient had been a schoolteacher, had no hobbies, and was not athletic in any way. At retirement, the part of her brain that she formerly used was no longer actively needed— and the rest of her brain had deteriorated from disuse.

I have heard that this awful thing happens to one-interest workers after they are no longer involved in what has occupied their minds for most of a lifetime. It may have been law, business, or farming. It even happens to the homemaker who has made this her whole life and then finds she has no one left for whom to "homemake."

The moral would seem to be to expand our interests beyond what it takes to make a living, while we can still do something about it. As a social-concern slogan goes: "A mind is a terrible thing to waste." Not even the most sophisticated computer can begin to compare with the brain God has built into us. In fact, how would there ever have been a computer except for man's brain that invented it!

In our preparation for retirement, as we save and plan for the future, one of the best pieces of planning will be keeping our minds alert. It will not matter that we have enough money or a comfortable home, if we become senile and dependent on other people's minds. Personally, there will never be enough time for me to read all the wonderful books or discuss myriad areas that interest me. I find that another fine mind stretcher is memorizing portions of the Bible. It is a challenge to fill my memory bank with such valuable material, and a good feeling to be able to recite to myself a chapter I have committed to memory. I would highly recommend this as a daily practice. The day might come when we will be thankful we did this while we still could. I get a little impatient with people who tell me they are too old to memorize. I taught a women's class for some years, and when I would urge them to memorize a chapter at a time with me, most of them would demur, using their age as the excuse. One day I was able to assure them that a mind is not like the top drawer of a dresser that holds so much and no more. This spoke to a number of them and together we did accomplish quite a bit of memorizing. Now, when the need arises, the Holy Spirit can bring to remembrance those verses we have deliberately committed to memory. Even the Spirit of God cannot bring to recollection something we have never learned.

Granted, some people have more facility than others. But God made us. He "knoweth our frame"—our strengths and our weaknesses (*see* Psalms 103:14). He will empower us to do those things that will keep us alert and fruitful. That we will still bring forth fruit in our old age is a definite promise in the Bible (Psalms 92:14). Isn't this a guarantee of some "best years" ahead?

Living in the Past

A sure deterrent to having a "best time of your life" is the propensity for living in the past. We can and do learn from the past, but it is self-defeating to let memories control the present. It is my comforting belief that God kindly broke time into segments for us so that we can have new beginnings. Every day is a fresh new page. Even if at nightfall I look over my day objectively and see where I have "left undone those things which I ought to have done, and done those things which I ought not to have done" (*see* "A General Confession" in *The Book of Common Prayer*), there is something I can do about it. Right now I am memorizing the Book of First John and this verse comes to mind:

> If we confess our sins, he is faithful and just to forgive us our sins, and to cleanse us from all unrighteousness.
>
> 1 John 1:9

That takes care of today's sheet with its blots. And I have a brand-new tomorrow ahead of me!

We can learn a lesson from the merchant world. Why do stores make such a production of their yearly inventory routine? To give you and me a chance to paw through the high-piled merchandise as we jostle each other at the sales counters? Not really. They have a dual purpose in their inventory extravaganzas: one, to scrap the no-longer profitable merchandise; two, to make room for new items. I can't imagine that the department heads get together to moan over what they might have done more profitably through the year. It is my guess that they are thinking of next year and how they can improve their performances.

It is likewise profitable for us to take inventory, not just once a year (though that can be a major stock-taking time), but daily, weekly, monthly. However, I am thinking of a healthy recall, rather than a possibly neurotic "beating oneself over the head" with such words as the poet Whittier wrote: "For of all sad words of tongue or pen, The saddest are these: 'It might have been.' "

True, we all have moments when we harbor such a thought. There is nothing wrong with dwelling on what might have been, or what once was and can never be again. We would be less than human if such pondering were not a part of our thought processes. It is the *over*-dwelling on mournful thoughts which robs the person of today's joy and prospects for happiness. It is my thinking that the demons must have a special mission to stir up people's minds and make us focus on remorse over yesterday.

One area of concentrating on the past which is particularly self-destructive is letting ourselves think of former hurts and those who have been responsible for them. In this department we need to have a complete cleanout. If there is one theme in the Bible that I would like to stress more than any other, it is this: *forgive and forget.* The past *is* past; it can never be rerun. What we did or did not do and what others did to us should not be permitted to cast dark shadows over the present and the future. And what's more, this is something we do to ourselves. I never get tired writing about forgiveness, for it is the most liberating theme in the Bible. We rob ourselves when we will not forgive another person. (Perhaps I should recommend that you read the chapter "But 490 Times, Lord!" in my book *The Image of Joy.*)

I find as I speak to groups in various parts of our country and abroad that people are hung up on this matter of forgiveness. Seem-

ingly we are passing over something that Jesus made a big thing of
—take a look at the Lord's Prayer. Then read on. Jesus gives a
postscript. On what point? *Forgiveness.* The Matthew version of the
prayer takes only five verses and then our Lord underscores forgiveness in two more verses. (*See* Matthew 6:9–15.) That is how important
forgiveness is! I get more little thank-you responses on this topic than
on anything else I might mention in the course of a thirty-minute talk.
Amazingly, it seems to be a completely new insight to many people
I meet that they can *forgive themselves.* They can accept it that God
has forgiven them, but they seem to feel it will take a special dispensa-
tion from heaven for them to be able to forgive themselves for real or
imagined sins and shortcomings. So it is a special joy to me to share
with them that, having put our case into God's court and with Jesus
as our Advocate (*see* 1 John 2:1) we can freely forgive ourselves. What
a great feeling!

I know about this problem for it was mine, too, for some years.
However, I learned that part of accepting God's free pardon is going
all the way and letting it extend into forgiving myself. I do not know
how this works; I just know that it does. So if you have the problem
of feeling that you just cannot forgive yourself, may I suggest that you
sit down right now and make a list headed: THE THINGS I CAN NEVER
FORGIVE MYSELF FOR. Then, the list complete, sincerely in your heart
offer it up to God. Believe He is hearing you, *for He is.* Forgiveness
is God's "thing" if I may say so reverently. Then tear the paper into
scraps and get rid of it. Perhaps doing this little act will forever nail
down the forgiving of yourself. It might savor of the Muslims I've
heard of—who get rid of their sins by writing them on a slate, washing
the slate clean, and then drinking the water. Of course, this can never
really wash away their sins. And tearing up a list of things you cannot
forgive yourself for will not resolve the problem, but it just may direct
your heart and mind to the One who can give complete "forever"
forgiveness—even to empowering you to grant yourself pardon.

Nobody has to go through the rest of life filled with regrets over
the past. And nothing will more surely produce misery. It is sheer
futility to expend emotional energy on something that is beyond hope
of recall or change. Yet so many people, especially in the middle and
later years, let themselves be snared in this trap.

While we are taking inventory, let's take a look at our attitudes toward anything new. Are we rigid—not about to be convinced that something new can really be an improvement? If there is one thing more than any other that tends to infuriate younger people, it is the often smug attitude of their elders that says to them, "Things were better in our day. People were more virtuous, more ingenious, more thrifty, and above all, more thankful than you young people are today." Whatever the evidence pro and con, the subject is explosive. Filibustering on the issue merely creates resentment and builds gulfs where bridges are needed. Tolerance pays off (except, of course, in the matter of certain areas where we *should* be intolerant, but that is a topic all its own).

To enjoy a "best time of our lives," having rid ourselves of our stock of undesirable things, we can now replenish our lives with the good things for today and tomorrow. For a catalog of profitable personal items, let me draw your attention to a whole shelf of goodies. You will find them in Chapter 5 of Galatians: "shelves" numbered 22 and 23. The entire merchandise line is there. (It can turn us into a veritable fruit market—and what is more tempting to most people than luscious, perfect fruit!) Here it is: ". . . love, joy, peace, patience, kindness, goodness, faithfulness, gentleness, and self-control" (LB).

What a way to go!—as my pastor frequently says with his inveterate enthusiasm. And this is for *today*.

Frequently I come across a plaque with Robert Browning's well-known line, "The best is yet to be." Ultimately, for the Christian, this is undeniable. But the words have a faraway, sweet-by-and-by ring to them. For it is *today* that we need a "best" in our lives if we are going to put credibility in our future. And it is God's will that we enjoy today. He ". . . giveth us richly all things to enjoy" (1 Timothy 6:17), not to dream about for a tomorrow. To borrow a phrase from my British friends: "It's laid on" (meaning it is included in the provision —you reserve a room, and breakfast is "laid on").

- With the fixed attitude that this *can* be the most fruitful time of your life—
- With new communication and mutual understanding between husband and wife for the retirement years—

- With plans for not only keeping alive but also alert—
- With the past behind you, forgiven and forgotten, and a whole basketful of fruitful living offered to you—

You have it made!

The more we enjoy God's goodness *daily,* the more believable Christianity is to those around us. You can trust God to take care of your future, beginning with a generous slice of His best for you *today.*

14

Reclaimed—Redeemed—Recycled

For age is opportunity no less
Than youth itself.

Henry Wadsworth Longfellow

Drought descends like a blight on New York City. Stringent measures are taken to conserve water. Yet, at Lincoln Center and other public places, fountains continue to play their cooling spray, bringing refreshment to heat-weary city dwellers.

As though anticipating criticism, the Parks Department has placed a sign reading: THIS WATER IS BEING RECYCLED.

A group of keen teenagers collect, tie, and lug into a station wagon piles of old newspapers. Another team gathers empty cans and bottles. They have been at it most of the day and some of them look a little beat.

"What are you working so hard for?" a passerby inquires.

"To buy new band uniforms," the young people chorus back. "We're taking all this junk to the recycling plant to get money."

On a grander scale, Les Goldberg of the *Los Angeles Herald-Examiner* writes:

Old Phones Never Quit Ringing

When your telephone rings, the sound you hear probably has been recycled.

Higher new equipment costs are forcing the nation's major companies and suppliers to salvage everything they can.

And, what they can't salvage is being scrapped for conversion back to its raw material, and eventual reincarnation as other products. . . . A few years ago, it was considered cheaper to just "throw it away."

Recycling is a phenomenon of our recently affluent society that now —belatedly—sees itself as running out of natural resources. If recycling says anything, it is that the object to be recycled once had worth and someone has recognized this and reclaimed it from the scrap heap. Before recycling, however, must come *reclamation.*

Any item, no matter how valuable it once was, unless it is reclaimed from the trash heap, the garbage pile, the dump, will remain what it has become—a piece of junk. There is no hope for it apart from reclamation. It cannot pick itself up. Someone has to find it, recognize its value, and take a step toward reclaiming it.

I cannot resist sharing with you a chorus which used to be popular in evangelical circles. It went something like this: "Down in the dumps I'll never go; / That's where the devil keeps me low—" We were once singing this ditty at a children's summer camp, and later a boy about nine or ten asked with a disconsolate look, "Why is it bad to go to a dump? I get lots of nice things there." (Probably a young Edison.) This was before the days of recycling as we know it.

The Bible, always ahead of the times, recognizes the value of recycling human potential. But first—the reclaiming. David the Psalmist knew all about this. He speaks of being in a horrible pit and miry clay (Psalms 40:2). Doesn't that savor of a garbage pile, a trash heap?

But God didn't leave him there. "He brought me up," writes David. Not only that, but God "set my feet upon a rock and established my goings." As if that were not enough, David exults, "He put a new song in my mouth" (*see* v.3). Lifted out of misery and filth and uselessness —established, and with a heart to sing!

This is the kind of recycling in which God is interested. The greatest of all recycling jobs was done by God Himself. He recycled the dust of the ground and created man. He created good human beings—He *said* they were good. Of their own volition, the first man and woman spoiled God's good work; they became "bad." But God didn't toss them on the scrap heap. He gave them a way back. At no time in history did He consider it cheaper to just throw away a human being without giving him a chance. No matter how far or how low or how *anything* a human being has gone, there is no question that he originally had worth. He was made in the image of God. Lost as this was in Eden, nevertheless something of the image of God has been retained. Humans have always been other than only "animal."

When God steps in and reclaims a man or woman he is also asserting His prior claim. The person may have voluntarily gone over to the enemy's camp. But God has not abdicated.

Beyond reclaiming, there has to be *redeeming*. For example, we might know where certain items lie on the scrap heap. We might recognize that these once had worth and have designs on them for future use. But first the items must be bought. For the human being, the price has been paid. God sent His Son into the world to be the Saviour—the Redeemer of mankind. God lays claim and also redeems.

There is a heart-tugging story of a boy who painstakingly fashioned a little boat. He painted it, his mother made a sail for it, and with great pride the boy set it afloat at the edge of a river. He had a string on it, but a sudden gust of wind tore the string out of his hand and at the same time carried his boat into a current. In vain the boy tried by every means he could to recover his new boat. Finally, he had to drag himself home, almost in tears.

Weeks later, to his instant joy, he recognized his boat in the window of a secondhand-goods store. He dashed in, explained, and asked for the boat, only to be told by the proprietor that he couldn't have it unless he paid for it. That was sad news, for he had no money. However, after a while he earned the small amount and with unbounded delight reclaimed his prized boat.

"You're mine, little boat," he said joyously. "I made you; I lost you. But I bought you back. You're *mine.*"

It was none the less precious to the young owner, even though he had found it in a virtual junk shop.

Why would anyone reclaim—purchase—an object that once lay on the junk pile? We do this with the plan and design for *recycling* it. We have a purpose for the object. New York City could not afford "new" water; the salvaging teens had no money for their project; skyrocketing costs motivated the phone company. For all three groups recycling was the answer.

How much more has God a purpose when in grace and mercy He reclaims—and redeems us from sin! God has saved us "unto good works" (*see* Ephesians 2:10). A brand-new beginning. How many people throughout history have yearned for another start, a fresh new book with never a blot on it? And all the time it has been theirs for the asking.

Second Corinthians speaks of the new things that are a part of the reclaimed and redeemed life.

> When someone becomes a Christian he becomes a brand new person inside. He is not the same any more. A new life has begun!
> 2 Corinthians 5:17 LB

All things are new, the King James Version of this verse tells us: "Therefore if any man be in Christ, he is a new creature: old things are passed away; behold, all things are become new." There are new eyes to see, and new ears to hear what God has for us, a new goal of pleasing Him, new ambitions that go beyond selfish aspirations. Perhaps the most glorious of all the new things in one's basket of life after redemption is a new *destination.*

Everything new? It is almost too expansive a concept for us! I can get pretty excited over just one new thing: a new book, a new dress. In particular, a new friend or a new idea excites me. And here God is promising us all new things. God—who alone can keep every promise He ever makes.

Are you thinking, *I would settle for a new body, one without any aches or pains?* Fine! That is a part of God's package of new things for every one of us who will let Him reclaim and redeem us. The Bible makes it clear that we will have new bodies, indestructible bodies, a fact tied in with our new destination:

> [Jesus says:] "When everything is ready, then I will come and get you, so that you can always be with me where I am. . . ."
> John 14:3 LB

> When he [Jesus] comes back he will take these dying bodies of ours and change them into glorious bodies like his own. . . .
> Philippians 3:21 LB

But I am telling you this strange and wonderful secret . . . we
shall all be given new bodies! . . . the Christians who have died
will suddenly become alive, with new bodies that will never,
never die; and then we who are still alive shall suddenly have new
bodies too.

1 Corinthians 15:51, 52 LB

Tie all these definite promises into this—still another promise, and
one to which almost everyone who has ever lived can relate, and
which sufferers from physical ills can especially latch on to—Isaiah's
beautiful, hope-filled words: "And the inhabitant shall not say, I am
sick . . ." (Isaiah 33:24).

Despite great strides in medicine in our day, and although dedi-
cated researchers are giving their lives for the ideal of eradicating
human sickness and suffering, it is still but a dream. The inhabitants
of Planet Earth are still saying, "I am sick." But the day *is* coming
when freedom from suffering will become a reality. It is an integral
part of all things becoming new.

One of the wonderful aspects of all this newness is that it can begin
at any age. My children, for instance, were still very young—pre-
schoolers, in fact—when (probably because they had lived in an environment where the Bible, the church, and particularly Jesus Himself
were very real to them) each accepted Christ as Saviour—with the
pure understanding of a child.

My father, at the other end of the spectrum, was sixty-eight years
old when he came to Christ. To God this made no difference; His
mercy does not have an age limit. And lest you be thinking, as some
have, *I wouldn't want to offer my life to Christ at my age, when I've
neglected Him all the years of my life,* remember that for the sincere
person God has a solution for even this problem. "And I will restore
to you the years that the locust hath eaten . . ." (Joel 2:25). The
locusts: predators which rob and strip and leave utter desolation and
destruction in their wake! Only God can erase the wasted, destructive
time as if it had never been, and give you a chance to make up for the
lost years. So you must not let age deter you from being recycled by
God. Notice that I say, ". . . by God." He is the One who will do all
the recycling.

The most perfectly recycled being in the world is the person who has realized his worthlessness in his present condition. With this recognition, he has turned to His Maker, confessed his sins and short-comings, his dissatisfactions with what he is, and with what he sees as his future. God accepts him, forgives him, converts him—turns him around and makes him usable in His service and gives him new life that will never end.

Another few words about the matter of forgiveness—which we covered in the previous chapter. I am finding among Christians a rather strange anomaly. They appear to be able to accept and appropriate *God's* forgiveness, but they often cannot forgive *themselves.* As I speak at various luncheons and other functions, women come up to me or write little notes saying, "Thank you for helping me to see that I *can* forgive myself. This is something that has kept me from being a happy Christian."

The statistics are gloomy as to how many in their fifties or over actually turn to Christ for salvation and surrender themselves to Him for recycling. But God is never controlled by statistics. He does not have a shut-out age. His loving "whosoever will may come" rings in the ears of those who have an ear to hear, whatever their age.

In imagination I look ahead to a special spot in heaven where those who came late in the day will gather and rejoice together that they *did* come. The Bible has a great better-late-than-never story that I really enjoy. You can read it for yourself in Chapter 20 of Matthew. The parable is about a man who hired some day laborers for an agreed wage. Later in the day he saw some others standing around idle, so he hired them, saying, "Go to work for me and I'll give you whatever is right." Quitting time came and the men lined up for their money. And—the men who had started later in the day got exactly the same wage as those who had worked all day! Now, the eight-hour crew (or however many hours made a working day) received what they had contracted for. It took not one cent out of their pockets, that their employer chose to pay what he pleased to the latecomers. He was spending his own money. He was fair; he kept his bargain with the first group.

Another point to this story is that the latecomers were paid *first.* And, said the Storyteller, "This is like unto the kingdom of heaven."

No penalty there for coming late, for being fifty plus when you report for duty.

An encouraging parable? It is more than that. It is God's promise that He keeps the door open. But He doesn't push anyone through. Jesus said:

> Behold, I stand at the door, and knock: if any man hear my voice, and open the door, I will come in to him. . . .
>
> Revelation 3:20

This is the beginning of the recycling process. As an old hymn puts it:

> You must open the door, you must open the door;
> When Jesus comes in, He will save you from sin,
> But you must open the door.

"You Must Open the Door"   Composer: Homer A. Rodeheaver
                                Author: Ina Duley Ogdon
Copyright 1934 by Homer A. Rodeheaver.
© Renewal 1962, The Rodeheaver Co.
International Copyright Secured. Used by Permission.

God will never twist anyone's arm to steer him into His heaven. Jesus lovingly invites us and He will "present you faultless" before His Father in heaven (*see* Jude 24).

But I'm too sinful, some people think. They have a longing for peace with God and themselves. What keeps them from realizing this peace of heart and mind? They may be comparing themselves with someone whose life seems "perfect" to them. For such people there is good news: God does not grade on the curve!

I recently heard a business executive tell of his encounter with a colleague who apparently overrated this Christian executive as being "something of a saint." He was seeing himself and all his shortcomings and sins, then looking at the Christian and attributing to him only goodness and all the other virtues. To him these represented a ticket to heaven.

Allan, the Christian, had tried in many ways to overcome his colleague Fred's resistance (for the man was obviously dissatisfied with his present life). One day Allan hit on a solution. "Fred," he said, "you think you've committed too many sins—"

"Not 'I think'—I *know,*" Fred butted in.

Allan continued, "Well, let me tell you something. I've been doing a little figuring myself. No matter how hard I try, I'm committing sins, too. Even if I sin in just three ways a day, that would be over a thousand a year. You know I'm over fifty, and if for fifty years I've been sinning just three times a day, do you know how many sins that would total?"

Fred was showing evidence of getting the point. "I'd need my calculator," he parried, "but I can see it's a *lot* of sins."

It did not take long to convince Fred that God was not calculating sins; that He is in the business of offering salvation—forgiveness for every single sin Fred had ever committed in thought, in word, and in deed. He came to understand that God was not comparing one person's sin with another's, and that Jesus had died for all the sins of the world.

"*I* couldn't have died for your sins, Fred," Allan told him. "I have all these sins of my own."

Fred believed, and that was the beginning of "all things new" for him.

You are never too late and you are never too sinful for Jesus Christ to reclaim—redeem—and recycle you for all eternity.

The choice is yours.